ENGLISH CATHEDRALS

IN COLOUR

*A Collection of Colour
Photographs by*

A. F. KERSTING

*With an Introductory Text
and Notes on the Illustrations by*

C. L. S. LINNELL

LONDON

B. T. BATSFORD LTD

First Published, 1960

PRINTED IN THE NETHERLANDS
BY L. VAN LEER & CO LTD, LONDON AND AMSTERDAM
AND BOUND BY DORSTEL PRESS LTD, HARLOW, ESSEX
FOR THE PUBLISHERS
B. T. BATSFORD LTD.
4 FITZHARDINGE STREET, PORTMAN SQUARE, LONDON, W. 1

Faith in
Older People

Registered Charity SC038225
Registered Company SC32291?

21a Grosvenor Crescent
EDINBURGH EH12 5EL
Tel: 0131 346 7981

Email: info@fiop.org.uk
Website: fiop@dioceseofedinburgh.org

ENGLISH CATHEDRALS
IN COLOUR

CONTENTS

Page

Author's Note 7

I Cathedrals - their Origin, History and 9
Government

II List of English Cathedrals 21

III The Cathedral and its Surroundings 22

IV The Growth of Cathedral Architecture 26

V The Cathedral Builders 41

Map 47

The Illustrations 48

LIST OF ILLUSTRATIONS

	Page
Durham	49
Gloucester – The Lavatorium	51
Gloucester – The Lady Chapel	53
Wells	55
York Minster	57
Norwich	59
Lichfield	61
Lincoln – West front	63
Lincoln – The Angel Choir	65
Canterbury – South-east front	67
Canterbury – East end	69
Canterbury – Window in the North Aisle	71
Ely	73
Exeter – Towers from the S.E.	75
St Albans	77
Worcester – The Lady Chapel from the South Aisle	79
Worcester – The Crypt	81
Salisbury	83
Peterborough – West front	85
Peterborough – The Choir	87
Chichester	89
Winchester – Tower and nave from South	91
Winchester – Effigy of Bishop William of Waynflate	93
St Paul's – West front	95

Author's Note

The object of this book is to give a short introduction to the History of the Cathedral Churches of England, together with some information about their constitutions and government; also a few notes about their architectural development, illustrated in the pictures of the Cathedrals which follow, and enlarged upon in the commentaries.

In preparing the introductory part of this book I am much indebted, as all students of Cathedral History and Architecture must be, to Francis Bond's *Cathedral Churches of England and Wales* (Batsford, London 1912) and to Professor A. Hamilton Thompson's *Cathedral Churches of England* (S.P.C.K. London, 1925).

I am also most grateful for the help I have received from the Dean of Norwich (the Very Rev. Norman Hook); Canon H. Balmforth, Canon Residentiary and Chancellor of Exeter Cathedral; and Canon B. E. Foyster, Hon. Canon Emeritus of Peterborough.

C. L. S. LINNELL

Letheringsett,
Norfolk

Whitsuntide, 1959.

I Cathedrals: their Origin, History and Government

A church does not attain Cathedral status by reason of its size. Whether large or small it is a Cathedral if it contains the *Cathedra* or Bishop's Chair; the throne from which the Bishop exercises teaching, authority and pastoral care over his diocese or See (from *sedes* a seat); from the earliest times he was assisted and advised in his government by a council of priests who were 'fitted to him' as St. Ignatius, Bishop of Antioch, put it *c.* 110.A.D., 'as the strings to a harp'.

At first when Christians were a small and often bitterly persecuted minority they worshipped in private houses. In writing to the Christians at Rome *c.* 56 A.D. St. Paul sends greetings to the faithful in 'Aristobulus' household' and to 'the household of Narcissus' and tells the Corinthians about the same time how he 'baptised also the household of Stephanas'. The bishop's house was therefore the first Cathedral, where he lived together with his councillors, so that a bishop in early Christian times was in a similar position to that of the rector of a big town parish today living with his assistant curates in a clergy house.

But as time went on and Christians ceased to be persecuted and became more numerous, powerful and influential they emerged from their houses, which were no longer big enough for public worship; the buildings that were available and large enough to receive them were the *basilicas*, or law courts, which were long rectangular buildings (with or without aisles) one end of which was semi-circular (the apse), where there was a platform for the chair of the most important person, the *basileus*, the king or judge. When such buildings came to be adapted for Christian worship the chair (now the bishop's throne) was moved back against the wall and the altar table stood in the centre of the apse. In this arrangement the bishop's councillors, who, as St. Cyprian (Bishop of Carthage 248-258 A.D.) says 'were seated with him in the church', had their special places on either side of the throne round the curved end of the apse.

Such were the buildings which the early Christians adapted for worship and it was the same plan that was followed when they came to build new churches. Such was the design of church buildings in very many places, and the Normans followed it when they came to build Cathedral

9

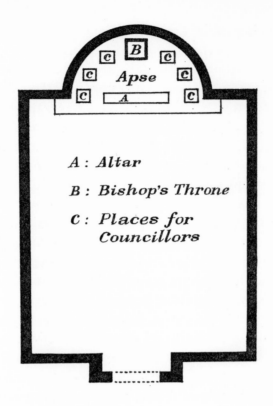

A : *Altar*

B : *Bishop's Throne*

C : *Places for Councillors*

Churches in England. But in only one English Cathedral does the ancient *Cathedra* survive; at Norwich, where the bishop's throne stands in the rounded apse directly behind the high altar with seats for members of the Cathedral clergy on either side.

In the Greco-Roman world in which the Christian Church grew up society was essentially urban, so that the diocese consisted of the local town or city and its surrounding countryside, with the result that even today there are far more Cathedrals and bishoprics in Southern Europe. But in the North towns were fewer, so that when the Christian Church became established in England the bishops made their headquarters, and Cathedrals were built, in those places which during the centuries of the Roman occupation had become towns after the Mediterranean model, e.g. Lincoln, York, Exeter.

Some of these old Roman towns were resettled by the Saxon invaders, but during the Saxon period the Christian Faith was in the missionary stage in England; this, and the fact that during the Danish invasions in the ninth century the Christian Faith almost entirely disappeared in many places, accounted for a very vague definition of diocesan boundaries, and Cathedrals were moved in some instances from one place to another. In the North the Cathedral at Lindisfarne was moved to Chester-le-Street and then to Durham, where the See was established in 995. In East Anglia the two Saxon Sees of Dunwich (for the South Folk) and Elmham (for the North Folk) were merged into the one See of Elmham, transferred to Thetford in 1075 and finally to Norwich in 1094.

For this reason, and also because when a diocese was very large the bishop might have a *Cathedra* in more than one church, some dioceses have a double title like that of Bath *and* Wells, and of the old diocese of Lichfield *and* Coventry; the principal church in each place (*e.g.* Wells Cathedral and Bath Abbey) having Cathedral status.

In modern times the fact that some places were the seat of Saxon bishoprics has been recalled by making them the titles for Bishops *Suffragan*, or assistants for diocesan bishops (*e.g.* Sherborne for Salisbury, Dorchester for Oxford, Crediton for Exeter and Thetford for Norwich), and some of them have in very recent times been revived as new dioceses (*e.g.* Leicester and Coventry).

As in Northern Europe dioceses were larger (*e.g.* the mediaeval diocese of Lincoln extended from the Humber to the Thames) the office of Archdeacon was developed to provide the bishop with assistance, especially with regard to the material affairs of the Church. Originally the Archdeacon was that member of the bishop's household responsible for the instruction of those who were training for the Ministry (and to this day it is the Archdeacon who presents the candidates to the bishop in the Ordination Service), but while he retained a place among the cathedral clergy his chief functions were in that part of the diocese allotted to his archdeaconry, and today he is often a town or country parish priest, though sometimes he is not engaged in parish work but holds a residentiary canonry in a Cathedral.

The word *canon* means one who lives under rule or whose name is entered on the roll of the church. The clergy of the bishop's household in early times lived according to a rule in which their functions were clearly defined, but when dioceses became so large that the bishop was no longer able to be present in his Cathedral except on occasions—and in addition to his diocesan work a bishop from Saxon times until the reformation in the sixteenth century was often a Minister of State—the Cathedral clergy became a Corporation, or Chapter, with an independence of its own. Its permanent head was the Dean and the Canons held certain offices connected with the Cathedral Church such as the Precentor, in charge of the music and the conduct of the services; the Treasurer, responsible for the possessions of the Cathedral and the administration of its endowments; and the Chancellor, who was in charge of the training of the clergy and ordination candidates, especially with regard to the study of Theology and Canon Law. Over the Chancellor's stall at Exeter appears the inscription *Hac qui sede sedes iura sacrata leges* (you who sit in this seat must read the sacred laws); and at Lincoln the Chancellor has the oversight of the Theological College which is called the *Scholae Cancellarii* (the Chancellor's School).

These officials would have their proper places assigned to them in the church and the usual arrangement was that the Precentor occupied the return stall at the north-west corner of the choir opposite to the Dean. Hence the names of the two sides of a choir, *decani*, the Dean's side, and *cantoris*, the Precentor's or Chanter's.

As time went on and Cathedral Churches attracted endowments the number of canons tended to increase and each had his *prebend*, or share, in the Cathedral's resources. For this reason canonries came to be named after the places in which the estates lay by which they were endowed: a custom which still continues though only in name, *e.g. Prebendary of Yatesbury* in Salisbury Cathedral; *Prebendary of Holborn* in St. Paul's; *Prebendary of Colwall* in Hereford Cathedral. In some Cathedrals (*e.g.* Lincoln) the names of the prebends survive above the stalls to which they were attached.

Though there were many local variations in the rules whereby Cathedral Chapters were governed the position was much the same everywhere. Chrodegang, Bishop of Metz, drew up a rule for the canons of his Cathedral in the ninth century and the constitutions of many English Cathedrals seem to have been of Continental origin. Giraldus Cambrensis (Gerald de Barri), Archdeacon of St. David's, who was at Lincoln from 1196 to 1199, says that Remigius, the first Bishop of Lincoln, followed the constitution of Rouen for his Cathedral, and in 1090 Archbishop Thomas of York followed that of Bayeux where he had been Treasurer.

It is to be emphasised however that canons living according to such rules where not monks but secular clergy living in the world. St. Augustine, the first Archbishop of Canterbury, who was a monk, and had been Abbot of the Benedictine monastery on the Coelian Hill in Rome, founded a Benedictine monastery at Canterbury that was called by his name, but it was distinct from the Cathedral that was established by him with a staff of secular canons. At York the Cathedral stands within the city walls and a Benedictine monastery was established outside as was the case at Paris, Rouen, Chartres and Le Mans.

On the Continent many of the older Cathedrals were established long before monasticism reached them, but in England some Cathedrals were not settled until Norman times, during the eleventh century, at a time when there was a tremendous growth and development of the monastic system. Thus many of the Norman Bishops, who were also monks like Archbishop Lanfranc of Canterbury and his successor Anselm, both of whom had been monks at the Benedictine monastery at Bec in Normandy, changed the government of their Cathedral Churches. Wherever possible they replaced the old Chapters of secular canons by a monastic Chapter, as did Lanfranc at Canterbury and at Rochester; and when Bishop Herbert de Losinga, who has been a monk at Fécamp, established his new Cathedral Church at Norwich in 1094 he provided for a Chapter of Benedictine monks.

The existence of monastic and secular Chapters resulted in there being two kinds of Cathedral Foundation in England. Before the Reformation in the sixteenth century nine Cathedrals were secular and eight monastic. With the dissolution of the monasteries in 1536 and 1539 the monastic Chapters were replaced by secular clergy and given new constitutions. Hence these are known as Cathedrals of the *New Foundation*, but the secular Cathedrals retained their old constitutions and are known as Cathedrals of the *Old Foundation*.

Some great churches, whether Cathedrals or not, are called *Minsters*, which is an Old English word for a monastery or for the church attached to a monastery. Thus York and Beverley, though called such, are not really Minsters as they were never monastic and the name is more correctly used at West*minster*, which was a monastic church, and in those places which owe their origin to a monastery, e.g. Leo*minster*.

When a monastic Chapter was established it was almost invariably of the Benedictine Order, but in one English Cathedral, Carlisle, the Chapter consisted of Augustinian Canons Regular, which was a Religious Order developed from the rule that St. Augustine (Bishop of Hippo in North Africa, 397-430 A.D.) had drawn up for the clergy of his household. At Carlisle however it was the monastery which preceded the Cathedral; the Priory Church there being founded in 1101 and created a Cathedral in 1133—one of the two new dioceses, Carlisle and Ely, created by the Normans.

The creation of the See of Ely and the reorganisation of Durham with a Chapter of the New Foundation, was intended not only for the efficiency of the Church but also for the defence of the Realm. At Durham the bishopric was united with the Earldom of Northumberland as a defence against the Scots, and the Bishop, like some of the Prince-Bishops of the Continent (e.g. Lausanne and Chur), ruled as a Viceroy over a Palatinate with civil and military as well as his episcopal powers. Hence his Castle (now part of Durham University) and Cathedral—which also gives the impression of being a fortress as well as a church, like the Fortress Cathedrals at Albi and Narbonne in South West France—stand adjacent to one another, and he possessed another stronghold on the Northumbrian-Scots border in Bamburgh Castle. The See of Ely was also intended as a stronghold in the Fens—the last surviving area of Saxon resistance—and the Bishop of Ely retained a civil jurisdiction, and was Judge of Assize in the Isle of Ely, until 1836, when Durham also was deprived of the privileges of a County Palatine.

Apart from the removal of the Norman Cathedral, set among the old Roman fortifications on the hill at Old Sarum, to Salisbury, where the superbly beautiful new Cathedral was commenced by Bishop Poore in 1220, no further changes took place in Cathedral establishment and government, or with regard to diocesan boundaries, from Norman times until the

Reformation in the sixteenth century. At that time some of the larger monastic establishments which were not Cathedrals were allowed to survive the dissolution of the monasteries as collegiate or parish churches and in 1541-2 six of these attained Cathedral status.

The Benedictine Abbeys at Chester, Peterborough and Gloucester became Cathedrals for new dioceses carved out of York and Lichfield, Lincoln and Worcester. Westminster Abbey, which was also a Benedictine Monastery, became a Cathedral for a new diocese of Westminster consisting of the County of Middlesex, with the exception of the town of Fulham where the Bishop of London had his Palace, but this lasted only for ten years (1543-1553). During the reign of Mary Tudor (1553-1558) it became a Benedictine monastery again until it achieved its present status as a Collegiate Church under Queen Elizabeth I in 1560.

The Augustinian monastery at Bristol became a Cathedral, but from 1836-1897 the diocese of Bristol was amalgamated with that of Gloucester. At Oxford the Augustinian Abbey of Oseney, of which barely a trace remains, became the Cathedral for a new diocese carved out of Lincoln, but in 1546 it was transferred to the Augustinian Church of St. Frideswide which Cardinal Wolsey had converted into the Chapel for his new college (Cardinal College afterwards Christ Church) in 1524. Christ Church, Oxford, therefore holds a unique position among English Cathedrals, its Dean being the head not only of a Cathedral Chapter but also of a University College.

During the Great Rebellion, Cathedral establishments were suppressed and many Cathedral Churches suffered extensive damage, as at Lichfield, where the central tower and most of the vaulted roof of the choir were brought down by Parliamentary gunfire when the town was besieged in 1646 and were rebuilt after the Restoration in 1660 by Bishop Hacket.

At that time many Cathedrals required much repair; but most remarkable of all restorations at the period was the entire rebuilding of St. Paul's, by Sir Christopher Wren, after the Great Fire of London in 1666. After nine years spent in preparing the various designs, the foundation stone was laid in 1675 and Wren lived to see the completion of his great work in 1710. The new Cathedral was smaller than Old St. Paul's, which was one of the largest of all the Cathedral Churches of England, and though traditional in plan was in a style which was entirely new for English church buildings and aroused as much controversy at the time as the design for the new Coventry Cathedral has today.

Only one other English Cathedral has a great octagonal area at the crossing in the centre: Ely, which is believed to have inspired Wren for his new work at St. Paul's. The Bishop of Ely, Dr. Matthew Wren, was Sir Christopher Wren's uncle, from whom he received, in 1662, his first architectural commission, for a new Chapel for Pembroke College, Cambridge; and in 1699 he designed a classical doorway to the north transept of Ely Cathedral.

During the nineteenth century radical reforms were made in Cathedral establishments. The revenues attached to prebendal stalls in those of the Old Foundation were diverted to other uses, such as the establishment of new parishes in large industrial towns, and chapters were formed in Cathedrals of the Old and New Foundation as they are today and consist of a Dean and three or perhaps four residentiary canons who are obliged to keep their periods of residence in the Cathedral. The other stalls were assigned to honorary, non-residentiary, canonries, still called prebends in Cathedrals of the Old Foundation, conferred by the bishop as a distinction upon prominent clergy in his diocese, who, together with the Dean and residentaries, form the Greater Chapter of the Cathedral Church.

Such reforms and the vast increase of population in the industrial areas of England during the nineteenth century resulted in the formation of further dioceses in which some large parish or collegiate church was given Cathedral status. In the case of a Collegiate Church, as at Manchester and at Ripon, which was governed by a Dean and Canons, a Chapter was already in being. In some cases where a monastic establishment had survived the dissolution of the monasteries as a parish church, as at Southwark and at St. Alban's, it was possible to endow a new Chapter consisting of a Dean and Canons as in the older Cathedrals; and this has also been achieved in the two entirely new Cathedrals at Liverpool and Truro.

In most of the modern 'Parish Church Cathedrals', however, means were not forthcoming to provide a capitular establishment of the usual pattern and they are governed in a different way; by a Provost instead of a Dean and a number of Honorary Canons; the Provost is assisted by one or more Chaplains, who are the assistant curates in the Cathedral Church, which usually retains its former parish.

Recent times have also seen the building of four entirely new Cathedral Churches. Truro, commenced in 1880 and completed in 1910, was designed by J. L. Pearson and represents one of the most notable works of the Gothic Revival. Guildford, designed by Sir Edward Maufe, and Coventry, which is to replace the Parish Church Cathedral destroyed during the late war, and for which Mr Basil Spence had produced a plan which is entirely new for a Cathedral Church of the twentieth century; and Liverpool, designed by Sir Giles Scott, which was commenced in 1910 and which when complete will be one of the largest and most impressive of all the Cathedral Churches of England.

First and foremost the Cathedral Church is the mother church for all the parishes in the diocese. As the care of all the churches is given to the bishop, who institutes his clergy to their parochial charges, so his Cathedral Church has an estate and dignity over and above all the other churches. It was this pre-eminence of the Cathedral Church, and the particular rights and privileges of its Chapter, which was emphasised in the Middle Ages—especially in Cathedrals of the Old Foundation—and often against the bishop himself; for instance at Lincoln in the thirteenth century, when the Chapter resisted the claim of the great reforming bishop, Robert Grosseteste, to hold a Visitation, which was only secured to the bishop after years of litigation and an appeal to Pope Innocent IV in 1245.

In the past also, when dioceses were much larger and many parishes were remote from the centre of the diocese, relationship between the Cathedral and parish church was difficult to realise. But today, when the vast improvements in communications have made the Cathedral accessible to every parish, Cathedrals are able to fulfil their function as the mother church for the whole diocese. The nave—the people's part of a church—of a Cathedral will be used several times during the year for great diocesan services, when congregations from town and country parishes, and members of Church Organisations, will meet together for worship.

Secondly, a Cathedral exists as a great church where the worship of God may be offered daily with all dignity and beauty. Music has always

17

been an accompaniment of Christian worship and through the centuries English Cathedrals have maintained a great choral tradition. In Cathedrals of the New Foundation all the members of the Chapter, who were of necessity monks, would be present and take part in the choral services. But in Cathedrals of the Old Foundation those prebendaries, or secular canons, who were not able to be present except on occasions, were required to provide deputies, or *Vicars*, to act for them in the choir office. In the courses of time the Vicars, who were later called Minor Canons, acquired rights and liberties of their own as a college or corporation within the Cathedral Establishment, as at St. Paul's, and often had special quarters assigned to them as in *The Vicars' Close* at Wells.

A distinction also grew up between those Vicars who were in Holy Orders—who often acted as schoolmasters for the choristers or as parish priests in charge of city churches near the Cathedral—and those who were not and whose duties were solely in the choir. Then, when organs came to be invented and used in churches during the latter part of the Middle Ages, the Choral Foundation would provide for an Organist as well as a Master of the Choristers who was often one of the Priest-Vicars. But in later times these two offices were combined, as at Lincoln Cathedral, where the composer William Byrd was Organist and Master of the Choristers from 1563—1572.

Choral Foundations were often supported in the same way as the prebends; the village of Ashby Puerorum, near Horncastle in Lincolnshire, is so named as the rectorial tithes in that place were appropriated for the support of the *pueri*, the choristers at Lincoln Cathedral.

In some instances Choral Foundations have been augmented by the endowments which were originally intended for the support of Chantries and Chantry Priests. In the Middle Ages a benefactor would often provide a Chantry Chapel where Mass would be said daily for the repose of his soul; and this provided an attractive and less arduous occupation for the mediaeval cleric. Chaucer commends the *Poure Persoun* who did not abandon his parish

> *And ran to London, unto seynt Poules*
> *To seken him a chaunterie for soules.*

18

In cases where there was a large number of such Chantry Chapels the priests serving them would form another college within the Cathedral Establishment—in the same way as with the Vicars-Choral—and have special quarters of their own, as at *St. William's College*, York.

Chantries as such were abolished in 1547, but the Act dissolving them provided that some of their endowments should be used 'toward the keeping of a grammar school or preaching, or for such godly intents and purposes.' Hence in those places were there is a *King's School*—of which that poor, unfortunate and sickly little boy, King Edward VI, is often alleged to be the founder—the name usually means that such educational foundation represents one of the few things that escaped the pillage of Church property and was allowed to continue during the reign of Edward VI.

In some cases Choral Foundations were taken to be such educational charities within the meaning of the Act, as at Lincoln, where the Chantry founded by Bishop Burghersh (1320-1342) provides for those members of the choir known as *The Burghersh Chanters*.

The reforms which took place in Cathedral Establishments during the nineteenth century also affected Choral Foundations. The Minor Canons were no longer Vicars for non-resident canons or prebendaries, but assistant clergy with clearly defined responsibilities with regard to the musical conduct of the services. Thus a typical Cathedral Establishment today in one of the older Cathedrals will provide for a Dean, three or perhaps four Residentiary Canons, and a Choral Foundation of two Minor Canons, Organist and Choir Master, six or eight Lay Clerks (Choirmen) and a dozen or more Choristers. There will also be two or more Vergers, and some Cathedral Foundations also provide places for a number of Bedesmen or pensioners, so rewarded after long years of service about the Cathedral and its premises. In those places where a boys' school has continued for centuries in connection with the Cathedral, the Establishment provides for a number of scholarships.

Cathedral Establishments today are in a very different position from that of 'the household of the Bishop' that they occupied in the early days of Christianity, but they still have an especial and important function in the life of the Church. With regard to the Bishop himself they are in a special position. They are subject to his Visitation, and one of the results of the controversy between King Henry I and Archbishop Anselm over the question of whether the Church (through the Pope and Archbishop) or the King should *invest* a Bishop with the insignia of his office (his staff and his ring), was to secure to Cathedral Chapters the right to elect their Bishop. But this right has rarely been exercised with freedom. In the Middle Ages, when many Bishops were also Ministers of State, the Crown would bring pressure to bear upon such elections and until the Reformation in the sixteenth century the Popes claimed, and often exercised, the right to *provide* Bishops for English Sees. Today, on the death or resignation of a Bishop, the Cathedral Chapter receives from the Crown a *congé d'élire* (charge to elect) followed by a *Letter Missive* telling them whom to elect, according to the form, prescribed by King Henry VIII.

In the Cathedral itself the canons hold such offices—Precentor, Chancellor, Treasurer, etc.—as they have always done, and in these days many of them are also engaged on some special work in the diocese at large; and in Cathedral Churches which are close to Universities some of the canonries are combined with Divinity Professorships. But, whatever their functions are in the work of the Church as scholars or administrators, as members of the Cathedral Establishment they are, together with the Dean, the trustees of those magnificent buildings which have played so large a part in the History of England and the Life of the Church in England.

II List of English Cathedrals
(Date of Foundation of See in brackets)

OLD FOUNDATION
(secular canons)

Chichester (1075)

Exeter (1046)

Hereford (676)

Lichfield (656)

Lincoln (1075)

London, St. Paul's (604)

Salisbury (1075)

Wells (909)

York (627)

NEW FOUNDATION
(monastic)

*Bath (1088). Benedictine

Bristol (1542). Augustinian

Canterbury (597). Benedictine

Carlisle (1133). Augustinian

Chester (1542). Benedictine

Durham (995). Benedictine

Ely (1109). Benedictine

Gloucester (1542). Benedictine

Norwich (1094). Benedictine

Oxford (1542). Augustinian

Peterborough (1542). Benedictine

Rochester (604). Benedictine

Winchester (662) Benedictine

Worcester (680). Benedictine

—

Westminster Abbey. Benedictine. A Cathedral 1543-1553

MODERN FOUNDATION
(formerly collegiate or parish churches)

Birmingham (1905). Parish Church

Blackburn (1926). Parish Church

Bradford (1920). Parish Church

Bury St. Edmunds (1914). Parish Church

Chelmsford (1914). Parish Church

Coventry (1918)

Derby (1927). Parish Church

Guildford (1927)

Leicester (1926). Parish Church

Liverpool (1880)

Manchester (1848). Collegiate Church

Newcastle (1882). Parish Church

Portsmouth (1927). Parish Church

Ripon (1836). Built for Augustinian Canons. Collegiate Church 1604-1836

Sheffield (1914). Parish Church

Southwark (1905). Built as an Augustinian Priory. Parish Church 1539-1905

Southwell (1884). Built for Secular Canons. Collegiate Church 1585-1884

St. Alban's (1877). Built as Benedictine Abbey. Parish Church 1539-1877

Truro (1877)

Wakefield (1888). Parish Church

* First Bishop of Bath *and* Wells 1244.

III   The Cathedral and its Surroundings

A particular feature of English Cathedrals is that nearly all of them, monastic or secular, with the exception of those of modern foundation which had always been parish churches, are set within a clearly defined precinct or close. Such seclusion was necessary for a monastic church, but in many monastic churches the general public had the right to use the nave, which was often the cause of endless quarrels and disputes, as at Wymondham in Norfolk, so that some monasteries (e.g. Bury St. Edmunds and Castle Acre) found it expedient to go to the expense of building a wholly separate church for the lay folk in a different place.

But the fact that the public retained the right to use the nave in many places is evidenced by the fact that this part remained as a parish church when the monastic choir was destroyed (e.g. Wymondham, Binham, Malmesbury, Thorney and many other places). In some places the parish preferred to relinquish the nave and retain the choir (e.g. Boxgrove and Pershore) and sometimes, if the monastery was situate in a town and was the only church, the parish succeeded in retaining the whole of the church building.

But clearly at no time was it possible to exclude the public from a church which, though monastic, was also the Cathedral Church of the diocese. In such cases the parts of the precinct into which the people might and might not go was very clearly defined, as at Norwich where two gates exist in the western precinct wall: the Erpingham Gate, directly opposite to the west front of the Cathedral, and the Ethelbert Gate, which was the main entrance to the monastery standing a little further away to the south.

A secular Cathedral would not require such seclusion and many secular Cathedrals on the Continent stand in the middle of a town with its traffic surging right up to the doors. But in England Bishops with Cathedrals of the Old Foundation sought to obtain such seclusion for their palaces and for the residences of the canons. This was often difficult to establish, as at Wells and at Lichfield where Bishop Burwell and Bishop Langton obtained from the Crown, in 1286 and 1299, licences to *crenellate* (fortify with battlements) a precinct wall as a prominent layman might do for his castle or manor house; a wall in which, as in a monastic precinct, there would be certain specified entrances like the Exchequer Gate at Lincoln.

In some cases this was done for fear of armed attack, as at Hereford where the canons were afraid that invaders from over the Welsh Marches would plunder the Shrine of St. Thomas Cantilupe. More often the seclusion was desired not only for the residences of the capitular body but also to protect the Cathedral and its surrounding yard from becoming a highway and a fair ground. But this was not always achieved and time and again the very nave itself of Old St. Paul's became a passage way and a market. The commercialism which has destroyed the calm of many a Cathedral Close in the twentieth century is not something new in Cathedral history.

In walking round a Cathedral and its Close the sort of buildings which surround it make abundantly clear whether it is of the Old or the New Foundation. Cloisters will be found in both, but in a monastic Cathedral the cloisters were always attached to the church and were the centre of the conventual buildings, and were often glazed as at Gloucester; in them the life and work of the monastery was carried on. Secular cloisters, however, though they may rival the monastic ones in architectural beauty, as at Wells and Salisbury, are but covered passage ways and in some cases quite irregular in shape, as at Chichester, or almost detached from the church, as at Lincoln, where the cloister forms a quadrangular gallery in front of the Chapter House and was linked to the north-west transept of the Cathedral by a narrow passage.

The Chapter House also is common to Cathedrals of the Old and New Foundation, but while in a monastic church it might be of great architectural merit its use was as a room in which the day-to-day business of the monastery was transacted. But in a secular Cathedral it was usually a far more spacious and splendid building, designed for assemblies of the whole Chapter, and was often the most elaborate of all the buildings adjacent to the Cathedral, as witness the inscription over the entrance to the Chapter House at York, completed *c.* 1320: *Ut rosa flos florum, sic est domus domorum* (as the rose is the flower of flowers, so is this the house of houses). The Chapter House was often polygonal in shape, with a vaulted roof springing from a central pillar, as at Wells, Lincoln and Salisbury, all of which date from the thirteenth century. But the most splendid Chapter

House of this kind was built for the monastic church at Westminster *c.* 1250.

At the dissolution of the monasteries many of the buildings which surrounded a monastic Cathedral were demolished as no longer required. Some, however, were retained and used for other purposes, like the Refectory at Chester, standing against the north range of the cloister, which was converted into a schoolroom. It is this demolition of monastic buildings which usually accounts for the fact that the Close of a monastic Cathedral of the New Foundation has often been built over with sixteenth, seventeenth, eighteenth-century and later dwelling houses crowded along the precinct wall and on the site of the conventual buildings, as at Norwich; while the Close of a secular Cathedral of the Old Foundation remains much as it was, like the wide expanse of the Close at Salisbury and at Wells and the smaller though equally distinct position of the Close at Lichfield; in these places the houses of the canons and of the important officials of the Chapter remain, as in *The Treasurer's House* at York.

The House, or Palace, for the Bishop, the most important official of all, was usually entirely separate and within a separate enclosure, as at Lincoln and at Wells. But in some instances, especially in Cathedrals of the Old Foundation where the Dean and Chapter were often jealous of their rights as an independent corporation and resentful of episcopal interference, the Bishop would reside more often at a house or castle belonging to the See some distance away: the Archbishop of Canterbury at Croydon (and for this reason Croydon is still a detached portion of the diocese of Canterbury) or at Lambeth; the Archbishop of York at Bishopthorpe; the Bishop of Durham at Bamburgh Castle or at Bishop Auckland; the Bishop of Winchester at Farnham Castle; the Bishop of Worcester at Hartlebury Castle; and the Bishops of Lincoln often lived in the episcopal residence at Buckden in Huntingdonshire, which was approximately the centre of the old diocese of Lincoln.

But in Cathedrals of the New Foundation which had been made monastic by the monk-bishops of Norman times, the bishop would often exercise a greater control over the affairs of the Chapter; this was particularly the case at Ely, where the Bishop was also in the position of Abbot; and in those Abbeys which became Cathedrals at the Reformation the

Abbot's Lodging became the Bishop's Palace, as at Peterborough and at Gloucester.

From the lay-out of the houses in the Close of a Cathedral of the New Foundation the plan of the monastic buildings can easily be deciphered, especially in those smaller places which have not been subject to modern development. Nowhere in England is this better illustrated than at Ely, where it is well worth the stiff climb to the top of the great west tower to look down on the arrangement of the buildings below.

On the north side the little country town comes right up to, but not within, the precinct wall, as it did in the Middle Ages, and away to the south lies a park which was the monastic enclosure with its special entrance through a great gate—The Ely Porta built in 1397. Directly beneath, and in the shadow of the Cathedral, the houses in the Close—or *The College* as it is called at Ely—are built upon, and in many cases out of, the former conventual buildings. The exact size of the cloister and the refectory can be seen from the extent of the Deanery Garden, and the Deanery itself (now the Bishop's House) was built out of the Guest Hall of the monastery. To the south of this lies the Prior's Lodging, with its exquisitely beautiful little chapel built by Alan of Walsingham for his friend Prior Crauden in 1324. The School Buildings, which form the western range, are the Monastic Guest House; and the houses for the residentiary canons to the east and along the inside of the north precinct wall are built out of the monastic Infirmary and the quarters formerly belonging to such officials as the Sacrist and the Almoner.

The number and the plan of the conventual buildings at Ely give an excellent idea of the extent of the great monastic Cathedrals of England; a walk round any one of these, as well as those of the great secular Cathedrals, shows how the precinct was laid out and intended to be a Liberty, a Small State, a Cathedral *City*—though this term has been extended to mean the whole town in which it is situate—with its own constitution and government for those who lived in and served a great Cathedral Church in the days when it was built.

IV   The Growth of Cathedral Architecture

Of the ancient Saxon Cathedrals little survives. At Hexham in Northumberland remains of the Saxon Church built by St. Wilfrid, Archbishop of York, in 674, can still be seen in the crypt beneath the nave of the existing Priory Church. It was one of the four churches in the ancient diocese of York (York, Lindisfarne, Hexham and Witherne) to attain Cathedral status, by order of Archbishop Theodore of Canterbury in 681, but was destroyed by the Danes in 875. Its east end terminated in an apse which still exists beneath the floor of the twelfth-century choir of the later monastic church where St. Wilfrid's *Cathedra* still stands. A similar basilican plan can also be seen in East Anglia in the remains of the Saxon Cathedral at Elmham, which was converted into a country house for the Bishops of Norwich in the later Middle Ages.

The rebuilding of the English Cathedrals, together with many monastic and parish churches, was the work of the Normans, that amazing race of men who dominated Western Europe from Scotland to Sicily for two hundred years; but it is in England that their architectural achievement can best be studied and appreciated. In England the Norman and the Gothic stand together as equals.

Always the rebuilding began with that part of the church which was required first, with the presbytery and choir, and worked westwards, the nave being gradually extended as funds permitted, as for instance at Peterborough, where the building of the great Norman Abbey Church occupied nearly seventy-six years (1117-1193). For the east ends of their churches the Normans frequently followed the apsidal, basilican plan, but in only three Cathedrals does this survive: at Peterborough, Norwich and Gloucester. At Peterborough the apse is only visible internally, its outer wall having been demolished to make room for the new building, or retro-choir, in the fifteenth century; but at Gloucester and at Norwich the semi-circular ambulatory remains right round the apse. At Norwich the *Cathedra* remains in its original position, but in other places the reconstruction of the east end necessitated its removal to the north or south side of the presbytery; now no longer a simple chair, but an impressive canopied throne, as at Exeter, where the throne, made for Bishop Stapledon (1308-1326), has a canopy fifty-seven feet high.

The removal of many a Norman apse was often necessitated by the building of a shrine directly behind the high altar. In early days the bodies of the saints were buried in a crypt beneath the altar, and crypts are a particular feature of Norman churches (e.g. the Norman east ends of Canterbury, Gloucester, Winchester and Worcester Cathedrals were raised over crypts), but the development of pilgrimages demanded that the shrine should be more accessible to vast numbers of pilgrims. The Shrines of St. Thomas Becket, St. Swithun, St. Wulfstan and St. Cuthbert necessitated the rebuilding of the east ends of Canterbury, Winchester, Worcester and Durham Cathedrals at the end of the twelfth and during the first half of the thirteenth century. But the most remarkable of such reconstructions was at Ely, where in place of the old Norman apse Bishop Hugh de Northwold built the superb presbytery (1235-1252), no less than six bays in length, to house the Shrine of St. Etheldreda.

At Gloucester and at Norwich, however, no such local cultus existed and so the old Norman east ends remained unaltered, and it is in these two Cathedrals and at Durham that the principles of Norman (Romanesque) construction can be studied as well as anywhere in England.

At Norwich the plan of the whole church remains practically unchanged. Nave, aisles, transepts, presbytery, remain almost exactly as when they were built between the years 1096 and 1145. The ground floor arches are low as it was intended, as in many big Norman churches, to bring most of the light not through the aisle windows but through the lofty triforium (*trifoire* meaning 'pierced wall') above; and at the top, a narrow clerestory. Thus Norwich is in marked contrast to Gloucester, where the Norman pillars in the nave are some of the tallest in existence and the height of the nave arcade is greater than that of the triforium and clerestory put together. Norwich therefore represents one form of Norman design which is repeated at Ely, Peterborough and in the Benedictine Abbeys of Wymondham and Binham in Norfolk and has its counterpart in Normandy at Jumièges and in the Abbaye-aux-hommes at Caen. Gloucester is the most splendid example of another West Country type of Norman work, which can also be seen in the neighbouring Benedictine Abbeys at Tewkesbury and Pershore and which is quite distinct from anything of the period that can be seen in Normandy.

But if at Gloucester and at Norwich it is the Norman plan and design which is impressive it is Durham in particular which reveals the vigour of Norman engineering. Durham is much wider than the other Norman Cathedrals, making the construction of the roof more difficult, and for this reason many Norman churches were narrow, as at Norwich. In most places they had to be content with a wooden roof over the nave, but for a narrow aisle a simple vault was made consisting of two semi-circular arches diagonally across each compartment, or bay, and crossing each other in the centre. At Durham a vault of this nature was built across the great width of the presbytery between 1100 and 1105. It was subsequently taken down and rebuilt in the thirteenth century, but the lessons learnt from it are exemplified in the vault that was built over the nave a few years later and completed in 1133.

The cross ribs of the nave vault, running diagonally across each bay, are still semi-circles, but the transverse arches between them are pointed. A semi-circular arch is limited by the span of the roof. It will exercise a big outward thrust and tend to crack at the apex and in the shoulders if too great weight is placed upon it. But a pointed one will bring the weight downwards rather than outwards and it can be adapted to suit the span. At Durham the use of the two kinds of arch in the same roof shows how the Normans solved their greatest engineering problem, and it is the earliest example of the way in which by the use of the pointed arch and the vault the Romanesque developed into the Gothic.

Builders were not slow in developing the principle of the pointed arch and the vault. When the choir and presbytery of Canterbury Cathedral were rebuilt after a fire in 1174 the work was more slender than at Durham fifty years before. By developing the pointed arch they found that it was not necessary to make the pillars so massive and, provided the walls were strong at the points from which the vaulting ribs sprang, larger windows could be afforded in the intervening spaces with safety. Provided also that the arches were buttressed at the points of their springing, the roof would be just as secure, and eventually 'flying buttresses' were built from these points over the aisle roofs and down to the aisle buttresses, thus stepping the weight down to the ground by easy stages. Vaults could be lightened and yet remain none the less effective. *Lierne* ribs came to be used which, running between the main ridge ribs, distributed the thrust evenly between them, as with the marvellous vaults with which Cardinal Beaufort and Bishop William of Waynflete and Bishops Lyhart, Goldwell and Nykke, roofed Winchester and Norwich Cathedrals in the fifteenth century. Eventually, with the full development of the pointed arch, the late Gothic building became one in which the walls were nearly all window, with spender columns, and the vaults spreading out fan-wise from their springing as at King's College Chapel, Cambridge, and at Bath Abbey, which was the last great church to be undertaken during the Middle Ages. (It was begun by Bishop King in 1495, unfinished at the time of the Reformation, and not completed until the seventeenth century during the episcopate of Bishop Montagu, 1608-1616).

The vaulted roofs of the great Cathedral Churches are therefore not just ornamental, but were the most practical way of making a solid roof, and are a wonderful example of the strength that comes from accurate poise and a marvellous testimony of the originality of engineering skill of the Gothic age; all proceeding from the invention that was made at Durham at the beginning of the twelfth century.

A vaulted roof was also a valuable protection against fire, which time and again destroyed the wooden roofs of the older Norman Cathedrals and did immense damage at York as late as the nineteenth century, in 1829 and 1841. But here the nave, choir, and presbytery are of such width (forty-five feet) that not even the structural originality of the Middle Ages dared venture a stone vault.

Other disasters besides fire befell many of the Norman Cathedrals. Sometimes the weight of a tower would prove too much for the semi-circular arches which supported it, as at Ely, where the central tower fell in 1322, destroying much of the choir, and so gave that architectural genius, Alan of Walsingham, the opportunity of designing the wonderful octagonal lantern which took twenty years to build (it was completed in 1342); and which makes Ely one of the most amazing and beautiful Gothic buildings in the world. The span which it covers (seventy-seven feet) is far too wide for a stone vault and so eight huge pillars support a wooden spire rising to the lantern in the centre, the vertical angle posts of which are eight oaks each sixty three feet long and for which Alan of Walsingham had to search England. And at the same time as this tremendous work was proceeding the monks of Ely were also building their superbly beautiful Lady Chapel, which stands not at the east end of the Cathedral, which was the usual position, but at the north-west corner, as in the neighbouring Benedictine Abbeys at Peterborough and Romsey. The sculptured decoration of the canopies of the seats all round the walls, which represent the scriptural and legendary history of the Blessed Virgin Mary, are unsurpassed and the vaulted roof is one of the most amazing feats of Gothic engineering in England, for the vault itself is very flat and supported by a minimum of wall and buttress.

In an age which is much concerned with money it is interesting to recollect how much these things cost. Hugh de Northwold's presbytery at Ely cost £5040, or a good deal more than £100,000 of our money; and for the new lantern, choir and Lady Chapel, all of which were being built at the same time, the cost must have been far greater. This is only one instance. Works of equal magnitude were going on at the same time all over the country. Not only must the resources of the great churches have been vast, but the sacrifices made by a large number of unknown people must also have been very considerable; in many cases such offerings were in the form of gifts made at some famous shrine. Hence the zeal with which Cathedral bodies set about providing such a centre of pilgrimage in their churches; like the Canons of Hereford, who in 1320 procured at vast expense the canonisation of Thomas Cantilupe (Bishop of Hereford 1275-1282), after which a shrine was built and the east end of the Cathedral reconstructed by Cantilupe's successor in the See, Bishop Swinfield.

Two such reconstructions of great Norman churches must be considered by themselves in marked contrast to all the others: the rebuilding of the choir at Canterbury after the great fire of 1174, and the rebuilding of Westminster Abbey during the following century by King Henry III. In both these churches the design was essentially French, and at Canterbury, where a French architect, William of Sens, was employed, the work is very similar to that at Sens itself, which was begun in 1140. Five years after he had started his work at Canterbury William of Sens was injured by a fall from the scaffolding and had to resign, but the work was continued by an English master builder still according to the French design.

Canterbury and Westminster are therefore special examples of that transition from the Romanesque into the Gothic which was going on in other places in a more conservative way in the adapting of earlier buildings: in the alterations which were being made to the nave and choir at Hereford between 1110 and 1145; at Chichester after a great fire in 1186; and in the western porches added to many a Norman church at the beginning of the twelfth century, as at Durham (which was also used as a chapel) and at Ely. A porch in this position was often called a *Galilee*, for the *outsiders*, in scriptural allusion to 'the Galilee of the Gentiles', and on Easter Day the procession would advance to the west end of a great church with the words of the Risen Christ, 'I go before you into Galilee'.

Side chapels were also a feature of the great conventual churches, especially in those which were monastic, giving the monks who were in priests' Orders a large number of altars for their daily Masses. These were against the east walls of the transepts and opening out of the great eastern apse and were themselves apsidal, as is the case in the St. Edmund's and the St. Stephen's Chapels at Gloucester, and the St. Luke's and Jesus Chapels at Norwich. The most elaborate arrangement of this sort was at Westminister, where the ambulatory is encircled by apsidal chapels after the French fashion, as at Notre Dame and St. Denis.

In cases where the east end was rebuilt such chapels were also reconstructed, as at Durham with the Chapel of the Nine Altars which forms a transept across the east end of the Cathedral, repeating the arrangement which existed at Fountains Abbey (completed in 1247). But all these chapels were excelled in splendour by the Lady Chapels attached to most Cathedrals; they date from the thirteenth century, when the increased devotion to the Blessed Virgin Mary resulted in the establishment of 'Lady Masses' at which most of the Cathedral body would be present. Thus the Lady Chapel forms the largest of all the separate churches attached to and forming part of the great Cathedral or Abbey Church itse f.

It will be noticed that hitherto most of the examples of Cathedral rebuilding have been taken from the monastic Cathedrals. For a century and more after the Norman Conquest it was monasticism that was in the ascendant, but by the thirteenth century the secular Cathedrals of the Old Foundation had increased in influence and wealth with the result that many of these were altered and rebuilt even more extensively than the monastic churches.

One of the earliest and most remarkable of all such rebuildings was at Salisbury, where an entirely new Cathedral was built in about fifty years (1220-1270). As it was in a fresh position the builders were not hampered by the exigencies of site and the need to conform to the plan of an earlier building, so that Salisbury is unique among the mediaeval Cathedrals of England in being of one style throughout and is the most splendid example in the world of a great thirteenth-century Gothic church.

At the same time Lincoln also was being rebuilt. The Romanesque west front was retained when, in about 1220, nave, transepts and presbytery were reconstructed, culminating in 1280 with the Angel Choir (so called from the carved angels in the spandrils of the triforium arches), intended as a shrine for St. Hugh—Hugh of Avalon in Burgundy, (Bishop of Lincoln 1186-1200). The choir owes much to the design of Hugh de Northwold's work at Ely completed twenty years before.

At Exeter the two Romanesque towers, which are in an unusual position above the north and south transepts, were retained, but both the nave and choir were entirely rebuilt with the same purity of style as at Salisbury, but with greater richness of ornament, between 1270 and 1350. This great work was planned by Bishop Bronescombe, continued by his friend and successor in the See, Bishop Quivil, and completed by Bishops Stapledon and Grandisson. It maintains a wonderful continuity throughout, due perhaps in a large measure to the fact that Roger, Bishop Bronescome's Master-Builder, survived the Bishop by thirty years. The fact that there is no central tower gives a long, uninterrupted view of the vaulted roof from end to end.

But at Exeter, as elsewhere, the nave was divided from the choir by a solid stone screen, *pulpitum* or raised platform, built by Bishop Stapledon in 1325. The pulpitum was necessary in a great Cathedral or Collegiate Church, whether monastic or secular, because such a building is really two churches: the nave, the people's church, and the choir which is the church for the capitular body. The organ would be placed on top of the pulpitum, which is the best position for it; and one of the most deplorable things perpetrated by 'restorers' was the removal of this essential feature, as was done at Ely, Hereford, Lichfield, Peterborough and in many other places; and though at Exeter it was retained in 1875, Sir Gilbert Scott was made, much against his will, to remove the solid walls at the eastern side to give a view of the choir from the nave. The provision of such a *vista* from one end of the building to the other was the occasion of such mutilations, which, in cases where the pulpitum was removed altogether, makes the whole building seem narrow like a tunnel; and though by such means it appears as one large church, it is quite unpractical for worship; those in the nave may be made to hear the spoken word by means of amplifiers, but they are too remote from the altar and choir to witness and to take part in any service.

In those Cathedrals and other great churches where the pulpitum has been retained—and also in others where it has been removed—the function of the nave as a separate church has been emphasised by the restoration of the nave altar. This would have been even more marked in the Middle Ages, for in addition to the pulpitum there was also the Rood Screen, as in a parish church, standing one or two bays westward in the nave, as at St. Alban's, which is one of the few instances in a great conventual church where the Rood Screen (here built by Thomas de la Mare; Abbot, 1349-1396), remains; for the reason perhaps that the Abbey became a parish church at the reformation.

In Cathedral and collegiate churches the rood screens perished, but pulpita remained for the capitular body which required its own church, and they were sometimes splendidly rebuilt (as at Durham, by the Bishop, Nathaniel, Lord Crewe, in 1686, but afterwards destroyed in favour of a vista in the nineteenth century). In 1547 a Royal Injunction demanded the destruction everywhere of the rood beam carrying the great Crucifix (or Rood), with its attendant figures of the Blessed Virgin Mary and St. John the Evangelist, but in parish churches the rood screen itself was often retained as a result perhaps of the subsequent injunction, in 1552, and still printed in the Book of Common Prayer, that 'the Chancels shall remain as in times past'. Such was the devastation of those times that no church remains in which pulpitum and rood screen survive together.

During the thirteenth century the monastic Cathedral at Worcester was entirely rebuilt and the secular Cathedrals at Lichfield and at Wells so completely that hardly anything remains of the earlier building. Lich-field was begun *c.* 1200 and completed nearly two hundred years later with the shrine of St. Chad in 1386, the magnificent Lady Chapel being finished about fifty years earlier. Wells, begun *c.* 1180, was rebuilt in the usual way from east to west, the reconstruction culminating in the splendid west front embellished with figure sculpture which is the finest of its kind in England and was completed *c.* 1240, by which time work had already commenced on the famous retro-choir and Lady Chapel (completed in 1326).

At Carlisle, however, a great rebuilding which started *c.* 1220 was never completed. The choir and transepts were rebuilt, the former on a magnificent scale and terminating in a superb east window with as beautiful tracery as can be seen anywhere in England. But the Augustinian Canons were unable to afford a stone vault and they could not attempt a rebuilding of the Norman central tower, though a top storey was added, and they had to remain content with the old Norman nave. This was originally seven bays in length, but only two remain, the others having been destroyed during the Civil War to repair the City Walls. Thus Carlisle Cathedral has a rather squat and truncated appearance.

At the great Benedictine Cathedral at Winchester the Norman work remained until the fourteenth century, when, during the great rebuilding by Bishop Edington and his successor Bishop William of Wykeham, it was encased in the later work.

Of all the Gothic adaptions of Norman work Winchester is one of the most interesting, for not only was the earlier work used as a core for the later but much of it was incorporated in the later design. The Norman vaulting shafts were used and the triforium connected with the power arcade, thus providing a nave arcade of tremendous height. It is a most ingenious reconstruction, which was probably the work of William Wynford, William of Wykeham's Master Builder from 1394-1403, and whose name suggests that he came from Somerset; perhaps from one of the areas where freestone was quarried and where a master-builder could obtain his early training. A new clerestory was built above, but so extensive was the work at Winchester that it was not complete until late in the fifteenth century when the vaulted roofs were finished by Bishop William of Waynflete.

Winchester represents one of the latest of Cathedral reconstructions, but that which took longest was York. Here the work involved was so vast that the better part of three centuries were needed to complete it. The choir is far bigger than that of any other English Cathedral, and though the over-all length of the whole building is exceeded by Winchester the spaciousness of York is unsurpassed.

Remains of the Norman Cathedral, built by Archbishop Thomas of Bayeux in 1070, exist in the crypt beneath the choir. This, which was the third Cathedral Church at York since the foundation of the See in 627, was removed in 1154 by Archbishop Roger, who also built Ripon Cathedral; but his work was barely complete when the building of the present Cathedral began with the north and south transepts, which occupied thirty years (1230-1260). This part finished with the north transept, with its famous five-light lancet window, known as the Five Sisters; then in 1291 the old Norman nave was removed and the present nave, following the vast scale of the transepts, occupied the next fifty years and was complete in 1338. In 1361 Archbishop Thoresby pulled down Archbishop Roger's work of two hundred years earlier and began the present choir and Lady Chapel, which was completed with the great east window in 1408. The central tower was constructed between 1400 and 1423, and from 1433 to 1474 the two western towers were built on the foundations of Archbishop Roger's flanking towers at the west ends of the aisles. The great rebuilding, which commenced at the beginning of the thirteenth century, was complete.

The building of a central tower with two western towers at the ends of the aisles was the usual arrangement in Norman times, as at Southwell, where the three towers date from the beginning of the twelfth century. But in many places such towers were reconstructed at a later period, as at York, Lincoln, Lichfield and Canterbury; and the western towers of Westminster Abbey were not completed until 1745, to the design of Nicholas Hawksmoor, who was assistant to Wren and his successor as Surveyor to the Fabric.

Sometimes the plan of having two western towers was abandoned in favour of one great west tower, as at Ely and formerly at Hereford; a plan which was also followed at Wimborne and in the Benedictine Abbey of Wymondnam, where two Norman flanking towers were replaced by a great western tower at the end of the nave in the fifteenth century.

In Norman times the building of central towers had been a difficulty their great weight sometimes proved too much for the round arches which supported them. But in the narrow Norman Cathedral at Norwich such arches were able to support a tower of such strength and solidity as to allow a stone spire (the summit of which is 315 feet from the ground and second only to Salisbury in height) to be placed upon it in 1463.

With the development of the Gothic style mediaeval builders in raising towers took the principle of balance and poise, which had been learnt from the vault and the flying buttress, to its utmost limit; and nowhere is this better illustrated than at Salisbury. In 1320, a century after the new Cathedral was begun, two stories were added to the central tower, which had not been intended in the original plan, and on top of these a stone spire rising to a height of 404 feet from the ground. This was only possible by making the stone work of the upper stages of the tower and of the spire itself very thin and by propping it all round with enormous flying buttresses brought down right through the clerestory and triforium inside the church. But even then the builders thought it wise to leave their wooden scaffolding inside the spire, and in the fifteenth century it was found necessary, as at Canterbury and at Wells, to strengthen the crossing piers by stone girders and intersecting arches.

Salisbury tower and spire, though of such enormous height, blends admirably with the Cathedral as a whole and is considered by many to be the most beautiful and graceful steeple in the world, but one stands aghast at the incredible daring of the people who made it.

Many of the great central towers were altered, raised and embellished during the fifteenth century, as at Lincoln and at Canterbury and the beautiful West Country types at Worcester and at Gloucester, a design which is again repeated on a smaller scale at the Priory Church at Great Malvern. But such was the weight of a central tower that it was found unwise to add to the strain that it already exercised on the walls and pillars by putting into it a number of bells to be rung as a peal. For this reason bells were hung in one of the flanking towers, as at York, but where such towers did not exist a detached campanile, or bell tower, was sometimes provided, as at Chichester, built between the years 1411 and 1436. Detached bell towers of this type can also be seen near the parish churches at East Dereham in Norfolk and at Beccles in Suffolk, and one formerly stood to the south-west of Norwich Cathedral.

Along with the development of gothic architecture came the rise of other more specialised crafts, so that while in the early period ornamental sculpture is part of the architectural design itself, as time went on masons became more exclusively concerned with structural achievement, making as it were a frame of stone to be filled with the work of the carver in wood and stone and coloured by the glazier and the painter. But the works of these craftsmen, though specialised, were designed to blend with their architectural setting, as with the Chantry Chapels at Winchester for those bishops who had been responsible for the rebuilding; and with the great canopied tombs, like that at Exeter for Bishop Bronescombe and at Norwich for Bishop Goldwell.

The dependence of the more specialised craftsmen upon the work of the mason is particularly noticeable in the earlier period. Until the latter part of the thirteenth century the woodworker took his ideas both of design and construction from the mason. Their work was 'mason jointed'— dowelled together like stonework—and the design follows that of the masonry of the period, like the canopies of the thirteenth-century stalls at Winchester (one of the earliest examples of the way in which the woodworker copied the tracery which the mason executed in stone), which are almost exactly similar to the stone canopies above the tomb of Bishop Aquablanca (1270) at Hereford. The design is geometrical but when, half a century later, the masons began to develop the flowing, curvilinear, tracery, the woodworkers followed suit and found in so doing that wood could be used in this way even better than stone, but that it required to be treated and put together in a different way.

No longer was their work dowelled together in blocks, as if it were stone, but by adopting a framework into which the design could be built they achieved a lightness and grace which surpassed that of the stonemason, as with the wonderful late fourteenth-century canopied stalls at Lincoln and at Chester. By then it was the woodworker who was giving the lead to stonemason, as at Ely where the stone carving in Bishop Alcock's Chapel (1500) follows the design of the canopies of the fourteenth-century stalls.

Woodworkers also developed new ideas of construction, as in the fifteenth-century hammer-beam roofs over the north and south transepts at Ely: a design which can be seen to even greater effect in many of the huge fifteenth-century parish churches of East Anglia, and which was evolved as a means of bridging a wide span with a minimum of outward thrust and which is every whit as remarkable as the stone vault. In the way of structural daring and accuracy of poise the English heavy carpenters of the later Middle Ages showed themselves the equals of the stone-masons and their work is the most remarkable of its kind in the world. '*Si nous voulons voir les charpentes*', said Viollet-le-Duc, '*il faut aller en Angleterre.*'

As with the woodworker so with the glazier. At first he was compelled to make his design fit the tracery determined by the mason. By the fifteenth century 'he was', as F. H. Crossley put it, 'instrumental in helping to fashion the last great change in the architectural progression of the mediaeval period.' The great windows of the late gothic church, which architectural achievement had made possible, became frames in which the glazier could set his pictures, like the huge east window at York which contains 1,700 square feet of glass with over 120 pictures. Indeed York is made one of the most glorious of all the English Cathedrals because of its ancient glass; largely intact, it shows not only the development of the glazier's art through four centuries, but also the fact that stained glass was more than just an embellishment of Gothic architecture. No one can visit York without realising how essential it is to the great Gothic church. No architect would have built as the fifteenth century architects did if their windows could only have been filled with clear glass, as anyone will readily understand who has sat for some time in a large fifteenth-century parish church in the brilliant, unsatisfying and unrestful glare through the clear glass of a large east window which has been deprived of its colour.

Then the surfaces prepared by the art of the mason and the carpenter were embellished by that of the painter. Little remains of the paintings which covered the walls and roofs, but such works as the medallion pictures of angels which adorn the vault of the Chapel of the Guardian Angels at Winchester (*c.* 1250-60), and the picture of the Virgin and Child in the Bishop's Chapel at Chichester, executed at about the same time, give some idea of the splendour of this branch of mediaeval art. What remains is but a tiny fragment of such vast schemes of decoration as the painting of the nave roof at Peterborough (*c.* 1220); and at Ely, in 1336, where the Sacrist's Roll tells of how William Shank, Master-Painter, and Randulphus, 'gold beter for making gold leaf for Master Shank', were engaged to decorate the roof of the choir which had been rebuilt by Bishop Hotham.

As windows became larger the art of the glazier began to supercede that of the wall painter, since the pictures in the great stained glass windows took the place of the pictures on the walls, the area of which was much reduced as the builders developed the principle of the vault and the buttress. But it was during the fourteenth and fifteenth centuries that the mediaeval artist developed the art of painting on wood, of which perhaps the finest example in the world is the portrait (*c.* 1390) of King Richard II at Westminster. Norwich Cathedral possesses a series of panels (*c.* 1400), representing the Passion, which have been worked up into a reredos in the St. Luke's Chapel and in the St. Saviour's Chapel another series of panels, brought from the church of St. Michael-at-Plea in the City of Norwich, which represent some of the best examples in existence of the fifteenth-century school of East Anglian figure painting for which the rood screens of many Norfolk and Suffolk parish churches are famous.

Mediaeval figure sculpture has already been mentioned with regard to its setting in the architectural plan, as in the Lady Chapel at Ely and in the west front of Wells, and it can be studied to an even greater effect from the effigies on the tombs and monuments. Some of these are of wood, like the thirteenth-century effigy in Gloucester Cathedral of Robert, Duke of Normandy, the eldest son of the Conqueror, who died in 1134. Sometimes a wooden effigy was covered with silver plates, like that at Westminster for Henry V (1422), where the head was of solid silver. Sometimes they are of bronze, like the effigies of Henry III (1272) and his Queen, Eleanor of Castile (1292) at Westminster, the work of William Torel, and the effigy in Canterbury Cathedral of the Black Prince (1376), which is likely to be the work of John Orchard, who also executed the figure of the Black Prince's father, Edward III (1377) at Westminster: bronze effigies which were made by the *cire perdue* method; a wax effigy between the moulds which was melted out in the casting in the same way as in bell founding.

John Orchard was described as a 'latouner' and *latoun* or *latten*—a mixture of copper and tin—was extensively used in the making of monumental brasses. These can best be studied in the parish churches of England but the Cathedrals can supply some notable examples of this kind of engraved memorial, such as the brass at Hereford for Bishop Trilleck (1360); at St. Alban's for Abbot Thomas de la Mare (*c.* 1370); Eleanor de Bohun, Duchess of Gloucester, (1399), and Abbot John Estney (1498) at Westminster, and Bishop Goodrich (1554) at Ely.

In the earlier period stone effigies are often in high relief, like the Purbeck marble figures at Ely of Bishop Hugh de Northwold (1229-54) and his successor Bishop William de Kilkenny (1254-57). During the fourteenth and fifteenth centuries the use of alabaster revolutionised figure sculpture and tomb design, so that with the beautiful carving and exquistely chiselled features of such effigies as that of Edward II (1327) at Gloucester, Bishops Ralph de Shrewsbury (1363) and John Harewell (1386) at Wells, Bishop William of Wykeham (*c.* 1404) at Winchester and Archbishop Henry Chichele (*c.* 1443) at Canterbury, we have no mere conventional figure, as in earlier times, but the beginning of portraiture, for which alabaster was a far more sympathetic medium than stone.

A study of the building of English Cathedrals therefore might well begin, as I have tried to delineate it, with an appreciation of architectural form and design, leading into the work of the craftsman in wood and stone and glass and in painting, and ending with a study of those memorials from which, as time goes on, we begin to have the true likeness of those great founders and benefactors who caused all these beautiful things to be made.

V   The Cathedral Builders

THE great men whose effigies are on their monuments are commonly referred to as the builders of the Cathedrals, but while they were responsible for large benefactions, like the succession of munificent bishops and archbishops at Exeter and at York—benefactions which have made their names to be associated with the great works that were carried out in their days-it is not to be believed that they had the necessary technical knowledge or, if they had, the time to exercise it. Also, as has already been mentioned, a Cathedral Chapter was often jealous of its rights and was not likely to give the Bishop, or any other donor, an absolutely free hand in the planning of their church.

More often it was a Dean or Prior who was more intimately associated with the building and though there were churchmen, like Alan of Walsingham at Ely, who had a great knowledge of architecture; or specialists in some particular craft like Walter de Odyngton, a monk of Evesham who wrote in the thirteenth century the earliest known treatise on bell founding, and Walter de Colchester, a monk of St. Alban's whom the chronicler Matthew Paris describes as 'an incomparable painter', then, as now, Cathedral Chapters engaged trained architects to design and supervise the work.

But it must be remembered that such men were not architects in the present-day sense. They were professional men, but architecture had not yet emerged as a separate profession; they were Master Builders like John atte Greene, who executed Alan of Walsingham's marvellous idea for the Octagon at Ely. The Master Builder would be in charge of the whole work, having all the 'rough masons'—those who laid the foundations and built the walls,—all the 'freemasons'—those who carved the freestone,—and all the other craftsmen down to the humblest labourers, who quarried and carted the stone and mixed the lime and sand, under his direction, as the twelfth-century chronicler Gervase of Canterbury says was the rule there under William of Sens. (The dependence of all the craftsmen on the Master Builder is used by Dante in his *De Monarchia* as an analogy of the relationship between the spiritual and temporal powers of Christendom.)

A Master Builder was thus a person of considerable importance, and, like a leading architect of today, would probably have a number of buildings under his supervision; Cathedral Chapters would sometimes compete in securing his services, like the Dean and Chapter of York who persuaded a Master Builder, William Hyndlee, to come from Norwich, offering him a higher wage and indemnifying him against the costs of a breach of contract suit with his former employers.

As has been mentioned, the names of many Master Builders suggest that they came from those areas where freestone was quarried which often belonged to the Cathedrals, like the quarries at Bere in Dorset, which were the property of the Dean and Chapter of Exeter, and those at Barnack in Northamptonshire within the *soke*, or jurisdiction, of the Abbot of Peterborough and part of the Abbey estates. Such areas would also produce men specially knowledgeable in the use of their own local materials, like the 'alabasterers' of the Midlands, from Derbyshire, Nottinghamshire and Staffordshire.

It will also be realised that with great building schemes extending over very many years, and with the constant need for repairs, it was necessary for a Cathedral Chapter to have stonemasons and carpenters in their permanent employ; many benefactors gave legacies for this purpose rather than for any specific addition to the Cathedral Church. Benefactors were remembered in the Masses said specially for them, as in the *Works Chantry* in the south transept of Lincoln Cathedral.

It is clear too from the Fabric and Sacrist's Rolls at Exeter and at Ely that there were always one or more members of the Chapter regularly appointed to supervise building work and repair; in a monastic Cathedral one of the monks; in a secular Cathedral one of the residentiary canons, or perhaps one of the inferior clergy, who exercised the functions of a comptroller, whose business was administrative and financial and who often exercised in addition a judicial authority over the large number of craftsmen engaged.

It was the Master Builders of the Mediaeval period, and the men who worked under them, who made over the centuries a wonderful tradition of English building; a tradition which lasted for long after the Middle Ages had passed away. Local masons continued to build cottages and barns as they had always built them. In Cathedrals and in places where there were a number of mediaeval buildings needing constant repair,—and in some

42

places completion and extension,—there was need for men trained in the old ways; and it was on men like these that the professional architects of the later age had to rely. Men like Christopher Kempster, the Cotswold mason from Burford, whom Wren employed at St. Paul's.

It was only through the centuries, and with great buildings like Cathedral Churches were only a portion of the work took years to complete, that such a tradition could be built up; the lack of it was a gigantic difficulty for the Gothic Revival architects of the nineteenth century. With buildings so extensive as the Houses of Parliament and the Cathedral at Truro a tradition of craftsmanship, built up over the years among those engaged on that one building, was not available in other places. But true Gothic, as A. W. N. Pugin observed, is not made upon the architect's drawing board so much as in the mason's yard, and while information is available about the designs for mouldings and other features little is known about the working drawings (if any) made by the Master Builders of the Middle Ages.

The older builders did not stylise their work as *Gothic*. For them it was the most practical way of building a church to meet the requirements of their employers. After the sixteenth century these requirements had changed during the revolution that was, as Francis Bond so rightly says, brought about by means of the printed word. The great thirteenth-century Gothic church at Salisbury has the scintillating beauty of a written and illuminated service book. St. Paul's has the accuracy and grace of a neatly printed page. If the printed word made available new ideas in religion, it also meant that craftsmen were no longer Master Builders but the employees of professional architects who worked to book (Wren turned to architecture after a profound study of many sciences); who were themselves employed by people who required a church to be the same and yet different and furnished a little differently.

The Great Church of the Middle Ages, with its aisles, transepts, side chapels, is the Father's House in which there are many mansions—many rooms—but all gathered under the roof of the great room of the Church Catholic whose worship is centred in the altar which, whether at the high altar itself or at the altar of the smallest side chapel, is the Throne Room and Presence Chamber of the Most High. Wren's employers wanted a church in which the altar would still be in this all-important position and his design for this can be appreciated today as never before in the restoration of the east end of St. Paul's with the splendid altar and canopy above it, carried out by Mr Dykes Bower and completed in 1958.

But those who employed Wren also wanted a church building which would contain not only the ritual and music of worship (pruned and condensed into the Book of Common Prayer), but would also be a suitable auditorium for the spoken word necessitated by the greater emphasis that was put on scripture reading and preaching.

In building his Cathedral Wren was faced with the same mechanical and engineering problems as the Master Builders of the Middle Ages. He solved them in a new and a more academic way but with the assistance of men who had been trained under the old tradition. Thus his work is a wonderful blending of the old and new and it was built for a Cathedral body which had a continuous history right back to the earliest days of Christianity in England.

At the beginning of the sixteenth century this continuity of worship and of craftsmanship was influenced anew in a more intellectual direction. The sermons of Dean Colet at Old St. Paul's were imbued with the 'New Learning' which also makes itself felt in such works as the Italianiate carving in Bishop West's Chapel at Ely (1512) and in Henry VII's Chapel at Westminster where Henry VIII employed (between the years 1511 and 1518) the Italian artist Pietro Torrigiani to make his father's monument; and it is in the work of the monumental sculptor that we have the best examples of Renaissance and Baroque Art in England.

It is impossible not to feel almost in the presence of Bishop Lancelot Andrewes (to whom we owe the matchless prose of the Pentateuch and the Historical Books of the Old Testament in the Authorised Version of the Bible) 'still praying in his sleep' in his effigy at Southwark (1626). Those brought up with the words of the Catechism will feel very close to the author of them, Bishop John Overall, in the portrait bust in Norwich Cathedral (1619), erected by his *Secretarius Domesticus et Devotissimus Discipulus*, John Cosin, who in after years became Bishop of Durham. Unless you are prepared for it you get a nasty shock when turning into the south choir aisle at St. Paul's to be faced with Nicholas Stone's shrouded effigy of Dr. John Donne (1631) which, in the words of his friend Sir Henry Wotton, 'seems to breathe faintly and posterity shall look upon it as a kind of artificial miracle'. Salvaged from the wreck of Old St. Paul's the statue of Dr. Donne, Dean, Poet, and one of the most eloquent preachers the Church of England has ever known, stands in his shroud preaching an incredible sermon on mortality. The statue was made from a picture that was taken from the life as Dr. Donne was dying with his face 'turned towards the east from whence he expected the second coming of his and our Saviour Jesus'; and he was laid in a grave toward the west that he might behold Him whose Name is the Bright and Morning Star. *Hic licet in Occiduo Cinere Aspicit Eum Cujus Nomen est Oriens.*

Though the Renaissance sculptor achieved a new and moving realism, such inscriptions as this (which was composed by Dr. Donne himself) show the seventeenth century to be no less an age of emblems. In the Middle Ages the humblest of parish churches in which the nave was divided from the chancel by the rood screen, and in the greatest of Cathedrals divided into rooms with their screens, pulpitum and parcloses, and with the arcades, triforia and clerestories soaring to the vault above— like a forest glade in stone—all was designed to emphasise the mystery of worship. All branches of mediaeval art were employed in allegory and scriptural allusion to declare the doctrine of God's redeeming work among mankind and the teaching of the Church about man and his salvation, as in the wonderful series of roof bosses in Norwich Cathedral beginning with the Creation and ending with The Last Judgement.

In the seventeenth century also the whole building itself, as well as the Word that was said and sung in it, was to declare the Majesty and the Power of God.

The Arches built (like Hev'n) wide and high
Show His Magnificence and Majesty
Whose House it is: with so much Art and Cost
The Pile is fram'd, the curious Knobs embost,
Set off with Gold, that me it doth more pleas
Than Princes Courts and Royal Palaces;
Great Stones pil'd up by costly labors there

Like Mountains carv'd by human skill appear;
Where Towers, Pillars, Pinnacles and Spires
Do all concur to match my great desires,
Whose Joy it is to see such Structures rais'd
To th'end my God and Father should be prais'd.

Churches   *Thomas Traherne (1637-1674)*

But there is no reformation without revolution, which is so often accompanied by what Sir Thomas Browne called 'an inconsiderate Zeal' in which many beautiful things are destroyed. In the sixteenth century many Chantry Chapels were demolished and Rood Screens hewed down, but it must be remembered that the worst iconoclasm of the Reformation period came a century later during the Civil War. This is especially true of the Cathedrals, many of which were grievously damaged; one of the propositions presented by Parliament to King Charles I at Oxford in February 1642 was that they should be utterly abolished.

'Lord, what work was here' quoth Bishop Joseph Hall (a very gentle and dignified old man, one of those who always suffer most in revolutions) as he beheld the destruction wrought in his Cathedral Church at Norwich. 'What clattering of glasses! What beating down of walls! What tearing up of monuments! What pulling down of seats! What wresting out of irons and brass from the windows and graves! What defacing of arms! What demolishing of curious stone-work, that had not any representative in the world, but only the cost of the founder, and skill of the mason!'

But the 'skill of the mason' was still there and available for repair of so many of these things when better times came, and the great development in Church Art, which marked the Jacobean and Caroline period at the beginning of the seventeenth century, was resumed after the Restoration. As has been said, the mightiest work of those days was St. Paul's, which was the last great church to be built in the old ways and also the first of a new kind. By the end of the seventeenth century the gothic was almost superceded by the demand for a new kind of church building which the new ideas in worship, which had been developing over the last two centuries, had rendered necessary. The study of English Cathedrals must inevitably lead into a study of English Religion.

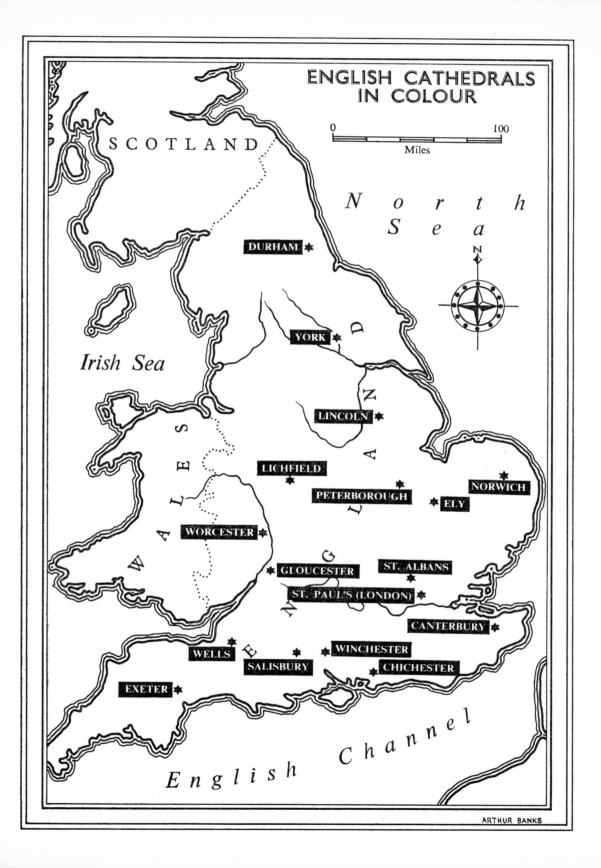

ENGLISH CATHEDRALS IN COLOUR

SCOTLAND

North Sea

0   100
Miles

Irish Sea

DURHAM

YORK

LINCOLN

WALES

LICHFIELD

PETERBOROUGH

ELY

NORWICH

WORCESTER

GLOUCESTER

ST. ALBANS

ST. PAUL'S (LONDON)

ENGLAND

CANTERBURY

WELLS

WINCHESTER

SALISBURY

CHICHESTER

EXETER

English Channel

ARTHUR BANKS

Durham

Cathedral Church of Christ and the Blessed Virgin Mary

TOWERING above the Wear, Durham is one of the most magnificently sited of all the English Cathedrals giving, as Dr. Johnson put it, an appearance of 'rocky solidity and indeterminate duration'. Adjoining is the Castle (now part of Durham University): a fortress as well as a Palace for the Bishop who in Norman times, and for long afterwards, exercised a palatine jurisdiction, with civil and military as well as his episcopal powers.

The Norman church was completed in 1133, but the two western towers did not have their top stages finished until early in the thirteenth century. The existing battlements and pinnacles date from *c.* 1780. Between the towers is the great west window of the nave, with curvilinear tracery. It was constructed in the fourteenth century and beneath it is the famous 'Galilee' Chapel commenced by Bishop Pudsey in 1176. He had originally intended to build a Lady Chapel at the east end of the Cathedral (the usual position), but, the site proving unsuitable, he had to put it in the narrow space between the west front and the precipice, thus blocking up the original west door. The Chapel consists of five aisles, the ornament of the arcades showing a marvellous blend between the solidity of the Romanesque and the lightness of the Gothic. It was altered in the thirteenth century and again by Cardinal Langely (1406–1437), whose tomb is at the east end of the centre aisle.

The enormous central tower (218 ft high) was built at the end of the fifteenth century and replaced an earlier thirteenth-century tower. Across the angles inside are built big recessed arches (called squinches), showing that it was originally designed to carry a spire.

Gloucester

Cathedral Church of St. Peter

THE Great Cloister at Gloucester represents the rebuilding of an earlier cloister and was completed in 1412 and is one of the earlier examples in England of fan vaulting. The illustration here is of the *Lavatorium* in the northern range where the monks washed their hands before going to their meals in the Refectory; the long trough being supplied with running water and opposite to it is the recess where the towels were kept. Just beyond this, and in a place now occupied by a window, was the entrance to the Refectory itself.

Along the southern range there are twenty *carrels*, or cubicles, for the monks. The Chapter House is approached from the eastern range and like the Great Cloister itself was rebuilt early in the fifteenth century and covered by fan vaulting. The earlier Chapter House, remains of which can be seen at the west end of the existing building, was built by Abbot Serlo (buried on the south side of the presbytery) in the eleventh century and was the place in which, according to tradition, William the Conqueror planned and gave orders for the making of Domesday Book.

At the northern end of the east range is a passage known as 'The Dark Entry', which led through into 'The Little Cloister' and the monastic Infirmary, and between the Chapter House and the north transept of the Church 'The Abbot's Cloister' and in the thickness of the wall between this and the Chapter House a stair leading up to the Chapter Library.

At the south end of the western range is a doorway leading into a passage, or Slype, in which much of the eleventh-century work remains. This was built against the north aisle and has an exterior doorway adjacent to the west front of the Church. It was originally used as 'the tradesman's entrance' where farm and dairy produce was brought for purchase by the monks.

Gloucester

The Lady Chapel

THE Lady Chapel, built between 1470 and 1490, is covered by a magnificent lierne vault and is a splendid example of late gothic construction which is more window than wall. Its building necessitated the removal of a small apsidal chapel which stood at the east end of the great Norman apse and ambulatory behind the high altar and flanked by the existing chapels of St. Edward and St. Edmund and St. Stephen.

Much of the original fifteenth-century glass remains in the east window of the Lady Chapel. Above the western entrance is a small chapel in a gallery behind which there is a passage, known as 'The Whispering Gallery', ingeniously contrived to connect the triforia on either side of the choir and across the great east window, but in such a way that its existence is not apparent behind the window when standing in the choir.

The great east window is one of the chief glories of Gloucester Cathedral and is one of the biggest Gothic windows in the world. Erected *c.* 1350 it is a War Memorial for those who fell at Crécy (1346) and at the Siege of Calais (1347). As the window is wider by six feet than the choir itself the two easternmost bays of the choir are splayed outwardly and the window has winged bays to give it additional strength.

The two monuments illustrated are against the north wall of the Lady Chapel. Judge Powell (*d.* 1713) is represented in his judicial robes and is one of the most impressive works of the noted sculptor Thomas Green of Camberwell, whose signature appears at the base of the monument to the right of the inscription panel. Next to it is the recumbent effigy of Mrs Elizabeth Williams, daughter of Miles Smith, Bishop of Gloucester, 'who religiously and peacefully migrated to the heavens' on 4th July 1622, aged only seventeen. Notice the figure of her child in swaddling clothes on the left-hand side of the table tomb. Opposite to this, against the south wall of the Lady Chapel, is the equally attractive memorial to Bishop Miles Smith's other daughter, Margery Clent (1623), represented kneeling at a prayer desk.

All these monuments are excellent examples of the interest and care that has been taken in recent years over post-reformation monuments; these at Gloucester being excellently well restored by the late Miss Janet Becker.

Wells

Cathedral Church of St. Andrew

THERE are four things which impress anyone who sees for the first time the magnificent west front of Wells Cathedral, commenced by Bishop Joscelin *c.* 1220. First, the splendour of the carving, the niches containing some of the finest mediaeval figure sculpture in England. Second, the apparent width, for here the western towers are not built over the aisles, as in so many other cathedrals, but against them in the form of a transept. Third, this west front is a little low and squat, but though Wells has one of the lowest roofs of all the English Cathedrals the west front would have appeared tall and imposing if spires had been added to the towers, as was probably the original design. The southern tower was carried up to its present height *c.* 1386 and the northern one about fifty years later. Fourth, the doorways seem small and insignificant, but it must be remembered that the Green in front (from which this illustration was taken) was originally the cemetery and the most important entrances to the Cathedral were through the north porch (set in the middle of the aisle) for the people, and through the cloister on the south for the capitular body.

The western range of the cloister (fifteenth century) can be seen to the left of this picture. The cloister has only three sides at Wells (there being no northern range), which shows very clearly how in a secular Cathedral the cloister was but a covered way leading to the Church, and not an important part of the conventual buildings as in a monastic foundation.

On the left is the covered gallery leading from the north transept above the Chain Gate into the Vicars' Close: a passage which extends from that by which the upper storey of the Chapter House is approached—the finest of all the Cathedral Chapter Houses in England. (Commenced *c.* 1290 and completed *c.* 1320).

Appearing above the centre of the façade is the central tower (completed *c.* 1320; but about twenty years later the piers supporting it had to be strengthened, towards the west and at the entrance to the nave by an ugly stone girder in the form of an arch carrying an inverted arch, and towards the east by a solid stone screen at the entrance to the choir).

One of the most beautiful features of Wells Cathedral is the fourteenth-century retro-choir, with its superb vaulting, between the presbytery and the Lady Chapel.

York

Cathedral Church of St. Peter

THIS view taken, taken from the south-choir aisle, shows the east end of the Lady Chapel commenced by John Thoresby, Archbishop of York 1352—73, with its marvellous east window containing the glass that was made in three years (1405—8) by the artist John Thornton of Coventry. The lights (each one of which is almost a yard square) represent, at the top, scenes from Genesis and, at the bottom, from Revelation. At the apex of the window is the figure of The Almighty holding a book open at the words *Ego Sum Alpha et Omega*.

Just below the east window, to the left of the Lady Chapel altar, stood the chantry for Archbishop Rotherham (1500) in a place now occupied by a fine post-reformation monument, with recumbent effigy in academic robes, for Archbishop Frewen (1664), who was given by his Puritan parents the curious Christian Name of *Accepted*. In a similar position on the other side of the altar is another monument, with reclining effigy, for Archbishop Sharp (1714); it is the work of the noted sculptor Francis Bird, who was the pupil of Grinling Gibbons and was employed by Wren at St. Paul's. The hangings of the altar itself, a glimpse of which can be seen in the picture, are beautiful examples of Stuart *crewel* work.

The Chapel in the foreground is dedicated to All Saints and is the Memorial Chapel of the Duke of Wellington's Regiment, which gave the fine modern wrought-iron screens. Just outside these, against the south wall, is a very pleasing memorial to Elizabeth Ennys (1585), one of Queen Elizabeth's ladies in waiting, and on the opposite side of the aisle, (just outside the picture ot the left) and near the high altar, another for John Dolben, Archbishop of York 1683—86, who as a young man was wounded at the battle of Marston Moor.

The vast reconstruction of the eastern arm of the Cathedral was undertaken not only so that the place where The Holy Sacrifice was offered 'should be especially rich in ornament', as the Archbishop and Chapter put it in 1361, but also to provide a Shrine for St. William, Archbishop of York, who was canonised in 1227.

Norwich

Cathedral Church of the Holy and Undivided Trinity

THIS view of Norwich Cathedral shows the transepts, apsidal east end, with the Jesus and St. Luke's Chapels flanking it on either side (which are round and also have apses), which, together with the nave and central tower, represents the Norman Cathedral built between 1096 and 1145 and practically unchanged in plan.

The great central tower—surely one of the most beautiful of all the Norman towers in England—had a wooden spire, but this was blown down in a hurricane in 1362 and destroyed the presbytery roof and clerestory. A new spire was built but this was again destroyed by lightning in 1463 when a serious fire did considerable damage to all the roofs, after which they were all replaced by stone vaults: the nave and choir by Bishop Lyhart in 1470, the Presbytery by Bishop Goldwell ten years later, and the transepts by Bishop Nykke in 1510. After the first disaster to the spire Bishop Percy built the new and lofty clerestory to the presbytery which was vaulted by Bishop Goldwell (who also built the existing stone spire) in 1480. This vault with its flying buttresses is one of the most wonderful pieces of Gothic engineering in England, which, together, with the clerestory, forms a lantern over the entire length of the presbytery, flooding it with light; the picture shows very clearly how this new work was superimposed on top of the original Norman work. Each one of the bosses on the inside of the vault bears Bishop Goldwell's rebus (a golden well head) and he himself is buried beneath a canopied tomb (with effigy) on the south side of the presbytery.

Between the years 1245 and 1257 Bishop Walter de Suffield built a Lady Chapel at the east end of the apse. This was demolished *c.* 1580 but remains of it can be seen just beneath the easternmost window of the clerestory. The existing chapel of St. Saviour, which stands on the same site but is very much smaller than the former Lady Chapel, was built in 1930. On the south side of St. Saviour's Chapel and near the east wall of the Chapel of St. Luke is *Life's Green* where Nurse Edith Cavell is buried.

Just beneath and to the south of the south transept is a glimpse of the Cloister, rebuilt between 1297 and 1430; the architectural development during the whole of this period can be appreciated by taking a walk round beginning along the east range, along the south, west and north ranges and then back into the Cathedral again through the magnificent Prior's Door (with canopies and figures) built *c.* 1312.

On the right-hand side of the picture is the Bishop's Palace among the trees and to the left, on the skyline, is the tower of St. Peter Mancroft, the largest and most splendid of all the thirty-six mediaeval parish churches in the City of Norwich.

Lichfield

Cathedral Church of St. Mary and St. Chad

OF Lichfield's famous spires the southern one (198 ft high) was completed in 1370 and the other two in the fifteenth century; the central one (258 ft) being entirely rebuilt after its destruction during the Civil War. The restoration began in 1662 and was completed seven years later. At that time also the whole Cathedral had to be re-roofed; the new nave roof being a little lower than the former one, as can be seen in the picture from the weather-mould against the western face of the central tower.

Between the two western towers can be seen the central façade with its great window. This western front was begun at the end of the thirteenth and at the beginning of the fourteenth century and was reconstructed by Sir Gilbert Scott (1877—1884). The façade is covered by tier upon tier of arcades with figures of kings and queens, apostles, saints and martyrs; the nineteenth century reconstruction allowed for the inclusion of a figure of that uncompromising Churchman and the most illustrious son of Lichfield, Dr. Samuel Johnson.

Lichfield is one of the smaller English Cathedrals and is built of the local dark red sandstone. It has been more drastically restored than any, in 1788 by Wyatt; and the restoration of the west front by Sir Gilbert Scott was extended to cover the whole building. A comprehensive scheme continued after Sir Gilbert Scott's death by J. Oldrid Scott.

Lincoln

Cathedral Church of St. Mary

WHEN Remigius, the first Bishop of Lincoln, moved his See from Dorchester (Oxfordshire) in 1074, 'He refused', as has been said in allusion to Psalm 78, 'the tabernacle of Birinus, and chose not the tribe of the South Angles, but chose the tribe of Lindsey, even the Hill of Lindum which he loved; and there he built his temple on high, and laid the foundations of it like the ground which hath been established for ever'. The picture shows the Cathedral in this commanding position on 'The Hill of Lindum' with mile upon mile of the eastern plains of Lincolnshire beyond.

From the west the building gives the impression of immense width for the façade, like Peterborough, extended right across and beyond the nave on either side, the actual width of the nave being shown by the position of the western towers. But here the façade (begun in 1141), half a century earlier than that at Peterborough, does not cover up but incorporates the earlier work, which can be seen in the centre with the semi-circular arches either side of the central porch. The earlier work can also be seen in the lower stages of the western towers, which were raised to their present height in the fifteenth century. In the picture the south-eastern tower almost eclipses the great central tower—the 'Tom Tower'—which is a good deal higher than the other two, and bigger than The Bell Harry, the great central tower of Canterbury. Its lower stages were built in the thirteenth century, after the fall of a former central tower in 1237, and extended to its present height (271 ft) in 1307. It is the highest of all the English Cathedral towers and contains a bell, 'Great Tom', weighing five and a half tons, and until 1548 was crowned with a wooden spire making the total height 525 ft, and over a hundred feet taller than the spire of Salisbury.

Lincoln

The Angel Choir

RICHARD of Gainsborough, who lies buried in the Cloister at Lincoln, designed the central tower and also the Angel Choir. The interior of the eastern end of this is shown in the picture with the great east window beneath which stood the altar of St. John the Baptist who was the Patron Saint of St. Hugh of Lincoln. This part of the building housed the Shrine of St. Hugh (remains of which can be seen in the centre of the picture beneath the easternmost arch) into which his body was translated in 1280, in which year the Angel Choir was dedicated in the presence of Edward I and his Queen, Eleanor of Castile, who died at Harby, near Lincoln, in 1292. Her body was embalmed and taken to Westminster Abbey for burial, but the viscera were interred here in the tomb which can be seen to the left of the picture. It is however a modern copy of the mediaeval tomb.

Note the extensive use of Purbeck marble in the shafts and capitals of the pillars; the angels, which give this part of the Cathedral its name, can be seen in the spandrels of the triforium arches, and above the easternmost pier on the north side is the small figure of the famous Lincoln Imp.

Remigius, the first Bishop of Lincoln, was reinterred in the Angel Choir on the north side of the sanctuary and in the north aisle were the chantries of Bishop Burghersh (1320—1342) and Bishop Fleming (1431), the founder of Lincoln College, Oxford. On the north side were the chantries of Nicholas de Cantilupe (1355), Bishop Russell (1494) and Bishop Longland (1547). Among the many monuments to be seen in this beautiful place there is one for Peter de Wint, the famous landscape painter.

Canterbury

Cathedral Church of Christ

THE picture shows a view of the eastern arm of Canterbury Cathedral taken from the south-east in that portion of the precinct which was the monks' cemetery. The central tower (235 ft high) is called The Bell Harry Tower, though it is sometimes referred to as The Angel Steeple as it replaced a former tower crowned with a gilded angel which was the first object seen by pilgrims to the Shrine of St. Thomas Becket. Though of Late Gothic design, the core of its lower walls is the original masonry of the Norman church commenced by Archbishop Lanfranc in 1070. The south-west tower, to the left of the picture, was completed by Prior Goldstone (1440—1452) at the west end of the south aisle of the nave, which, together with the nave itself, north aisle and western transepts were constructed between 1382 and 1400. The north-western tower—a copy of the south-western one—was not completed until 1834.

The exterior of the choir, together with the eastern transepts, (the south-eastern one appearing in the picture with the Chapel of St. Anselm set at an oblique angle to it, St. Andrew's Chapel being in a similar position on the north side) represents the rebuilding of Lanfranc's Choir by Priors Ernulf and Conrad between 1096 and 1126. The interior, however, represents the rebuilding by William of Sens after the great fire of 1174.

This rebuilding was continued by William of Sens' successor, the builder known as 'The English William', with an eastern chapel far bigger than the one which had been built half a century before by Conrad. Hence the new work (commenced in 1179) was tucked in alongside the Chapels of St. Andrew and St. Anselm (as shown in the picture).

Canterbury

The Corona or Becket's Crown

THE older chapel at the east end of the Choir built by Prior Conrad was that in which St. Thomas Becket had said his first Mass and it was this part of the building which was rebuilt by 'The English William' to contain his Shrine. All round the chapel is an ambulatory which terminates in a round building known as the Corona or Becket's Crown. The illustration shows a glimpse into this from the apsidal east end of the Shrine Chapel and across the ambulatory. Notice the simple groined vaults over the ambulatory with their zig-zag and billet ornament, an English design more in keeping with 'The English William' than with the Frenchman, William of Sens. Notice also the foliage moulding on the capitals to the pillars in the foreground. Those against the wall in the background have Purbeck marble shafts; an early example of this use of this material, which was employed nearly everywhere a little later on during the early years of the thirteenth century.

Against the east wall of the Corona is a thirteenth-century marble chair (shown in the picture) called St. Augustine's and in which every Archbishop of Canterbury is installed. Its original position was directly in front of the high altar.

Canterbury, the Cathedral Church not only of a diocese but of a province—the metropolis of a province (hence the Archbishop of Canterbury is styled *Primate of All England and Metropolitan*)—enshrines the History of England and the History of the Church in England in epitome: a vast building and so full of treasures, in architecture, sculpture, glass and monuments; a place to which, as Francis Bond so rightly says, 'every Englishman owes a pilgrimage'.

Canterbury

Thirteenth-Century Glass

IN the windows of the Shrine Chapel (now called The Trinity Chapel) are a series of thirteenth-century windows containing pictures in glass depicting the story of St. Thomas Becket. On the north side can be seen the pilgrims proceeding to Canterbury and a King, probably Henry II, in conversation with Benedict, the chronicler of the Miracles of Becket. Some of these miracles which occurred after his death are shown in the window illustrated here (at the east end of the north choir aisle of the Trinity Chapel): a series of pictures showing the sick being healed at the intercession of St. Thomas; a series which is continued in the windows of the south choir aisle and in the triforium above on the south side.

These windows are not unlike the marvellous series of Chartres Cathedral showing the martyrdom of Becket. Being the Champion of the Liberties of the Church the story of Becket's Life, Martyrdom and Miracles is represented in Church Art all over Europe throughout the mediaeval period. These windows at Canterbury, apart from being most interesting concerning the Iconography of St. Thomas of Canterbury, are some of the finest examples in England of the stained glass of the period.

Ely

Cathedral Church of the Holy and Undivided Trinity and St. Etheldreda

THIS view of the west front of Ely Cathedral taken from Palace Green, and showing the Bishop's Palace (built by Bishop Alcock, 1486—1500) on the right, gives a splendid impression the great west tower, which, together with its small flanking towers, was the final part of the work on the western part of this great church carried out during the episcopate of Bishop Ridel (1173—1189). The tower was carried up to the first row of battlements by Bishop Ridel's successor, Bishop Longchamp (1189—1197), and was originally surmounted by a spire which was taken down at the end of the fourteenth century when the exisiting top stage was constructed—the lantern, with its four small flanking towers, each one of which contains a spiral staircase; the south-eastern one being that which is used. This lantern had a spire of timber which was removed at the end of the eighteenth century. The rows of windows in the lower stages of the tower are interspersed with bands of arcading with mouldings of different kinds, the upper band consisting of circular openings with quatrefoils in the centre.

Beneath is the magnificent western 'Galilee' porch commenced during the episcopate of Bishop Eustace (1198—1215).

Of the western transepts with their flanking towers, the northern one was demolished at the end of the fourteenth century at the time the parish church of St. Cross was built. This building was a lean-to against the north aisle of the Cathedral and was pulled down in 1566, when the Lady Chapel was given to the parishioners instead, and which remained as the parish Church of Holy Trinity until quite recently. The southern transept, having become ruinous, was practically rebuilt in the middle of the nineteenth century. Like the central tower, both the transept and its flanking towers have bands of arcading adorned with mouldings. The south-western tower was once connected to the eastern tower of the Bishop's Palace by a covered way and the street which passed under it is still called 'The Gallery'.

72

Exeter

Cathedral Church of St. Peter

THIS view of Exeter Cathedral, taken from the south-east with the Bishop's Palace on the right, shows the two towers above the transepts which were begun *c.* 1114 during the episcopate of William Warelwast, a nephew of the Conqueror and third Bishop of Exeter. To the left of the picture, and flanking the southern tower, is the Chapter House, which achieved its present form, with its tall window with 'perpendicular' tracery, in 1412. To the right of this, and against the east wall of the tower, can be seen a glimpse of the Chapel of St. John the Baptist; the Chapel of St. Paul being in a similar position against the east wall of the northern tower. Both these chapels were part of the original twelfth-century design, but were rebuilt in the fourteenth century.

Note the magnificent eleventh-century arcading on the towers and the row of circular openings just beneath the string course level with the pinnacles of the buttresses (seen appearing above the Palace roof) which support the vaulted roof of the choir.

The southern tower contains thirteen bells, so that a ring of twelve can provide peals both in the major and minor scale. They make the heaviest ring of bells in the world. The great Tenor (72 cwt) was the gift of Bishop Grandisson (1327—69) and in the northern tower is an even heavier bell, Great Peter (125 cwt), given by Bishop Courtenay in 1484.

St. Alban's

MUCH of the building material at St. Alban's, including the fifteenth century Lady Chapel, is Roman. Bricks and tiles from the site of the Roman city of Verulamium. The Abbey Church, becoming parochial at the Reformation, had fallen into great decay by the nineteenth century, the great have being almost a total ruin, so the present Cathedral represents one of the great works of the Gothic Revival in England and was carried out by Lord Grimthorpe who himself designed much of the work including the west front shown in the accompanying illustration.

The very long nave (292 ft) was begun by Abbot Paul of Caen in 1077 and the west end was taken down rebuilt and extended in the fourteenth century after the fall of the five Norman bays on the south side. As at Norwich the choir extended into the nave westward of the crossing above which is the Norman central tower which was also part of Abbot Paul's design. St. Alban's Shrine was behind the high altar and to the east of this the Shrine of St. Amphibalus, a Welsh priest who, like Alban himself, suffered martyrdom in 303 during the persecution of the Church which took place during the reign of the Emperor Diocletian. Eastwards of St. Amphibalus' Shrine is the Lady Chapel begun in 1300 and completed in 1308.

Worcester

Cathedral Church of Christ and the Blessed Virgin Mary

BECAUSE the present choir and presbytery at Worcester are built over a crypt all that part of the building towards the east, the Retro-Choir and Lady Chapel illustrated here, which is beyond the apse of the crypt, is at a lower level. Note the extensive use of Purbeck marble in the shafts of the pillars in the foreground and to those supporting the triforium arches in the same manner as in the Angel Choir at Lincoln.

This part of Worcester Cathedral was begun *c.* 1224 and completed *c.* 1260 and was the work of Bishops Blois and Cantilupe who are buried before the altar in the Lady Chapel.

The latest addition to the Cathedral in the mediaeval period was the Chantry Chapel (1504) on the south side of the crossing of the eastern transept (near the place where this picture was taken) for Prince Arthur, elder brother of Henry VIII, who died at Ludlow Castle in 1502; the Chantry being provided above his tomb by his father, Henry VII.

Worcester

The Crypt

THE crypt, together with portions of the north wall of the nave and the eastern walls of the transepts, is all that remains of the Norman Church at Worcester begun by St. Wulfstan (one of the few Saxon Bishops who retained their Sees after the Norman Conquest) in 1084. The crypt itself was complete by 1029 and has, as this illustration shows, an apsidal east end like the choir which once existed above it but which was pulled down and rebuilt on a larger scale during the first half of the thirteenth century to house the Shrine of St. Wulfstan, canonised in 1203.

The crypt is a most interesting piece of Norman construction. The short pillars with their cushion capitals support a simple groined vault and the whole is divided into over a hundred compartments (of varying shape because of the curve of the apse) so as to keep the vault and the width of the semi-circular arches as small as possible on account of the tremendous weight above that they had to support.

In order to build the crypt St. Wulfstan had to pull down the Saxon Church built by St. Oswald in 983. It is said that he almost repented of destroying 'what the saints had wrought'. His body was buried before the altar in the crypt with that of St. Oswald, and for a time there lay between them the remanis of the not so holy King John, who died at Newark in 1216. But King John out of a generosity that was unusual in him, and perhaps out of a concern for the very questionable state of his soul, contributed very largely to the building of the new choir into which his remains were removed in 1260. His effigy—the earliest remaining effigy of an English Monarch—lies on a sixteenth-century table tomb.

Salisbury

Cathedral Church of St. Mary

THE grouping and the proportions of the various parts of the Cathedral at Salisbury are superb but some of its individual features are inferior to many, especially the west front which cannot be compared to the majesty of the western façades of Lincoln, Peterborough or Wells. The picture shows its beautiful setting in the biggest, yet one of the most retired, of all the closes which surround Cathedrals of the old (secular) foundation, and with the Cloister on the south side, the eastern range of which extends along from the west front. But though linked to the church at the west end of the south aisle and at the south eastern corner of the south transept, the cloister is, as in most of the secular Cathedrals, almost separate from the church itself and there is a space between its northern range and the south aisle of the nave.

Note the flying buttresses supporting the vaulted roof of the nave, especially those at the angle of the nave and transept which assist those inside the church in carrying the immense weight and thrust of the tower and spire.

All Gothic buildings, depending on the accuracy of balance and poise, need constant vigilance if they are to be kept in proper repair and safety and this is particularly true of Salisbury where the balance is so fine that so many of the principal supports—particularly those of the great central tower—appear almost alarmingly insufficient. Salisbury Cathedral was extensively restored in 1669 by Bishop Ward and again in the nineteenth century by Sir Gilbert Scott and Mr G. E. Street. The tower and spire were repaired by Sir Arthur Blomfield in 1898 and again in very recent times.

Peterborough

Cathedral Church of St. Peter

THE great west front (156 ft wide and with three great arches 82 ft high) was built by Abbot Acharius (1200—1210) around and across the old Norman façade and western towers. The earlier porch was retained, thus making the central arch much narrower than the other two. The existing porch, erected inside the centre arch and with a big window with 'perpendicular' tracery, is late fifteenth century.

The original design for the west front was for it to have four towers; two at the western ends of the aisles and flanking the nave, and two at the extremities of the façade. The south-western inner tower was, however, only carried up to the level of the nave roof. The other, which is thirteenth-century but has been extensively rebuilt, can be seen above the left-hand gable. This is the bell tower which once contained a ring of ten bells but now has only five. Originally there was a Norman central tower three stories high, but this proved too much for the pillars supporting it and it was taken down and rebuilt *c.* 1350 in its present form as a lantern of one storey. It was again reconstructed in 1883.

Of the spires which crown the towers flanking the façade, the southern one, with its cluster of small spires, was built *c.* 1350 and the northern one about a century later. Above the wheel windows in the gables are the figures of St. Peter, St. Paul and St. Andrew.

To the left of the picture can be seen the northern arm of the Norman transept, part of the great Norman Church commenced by Abbot John de Séez in 1116, consecrated by Bishop Grosseteste of Lincoln in 1237 and completed by Abbot Benedict in 1193.

Peterborough

The Choir

AS shown in the illustration, the high altar at Peterborough stands in the Norman apse the outer wall of which was demolished when the new east end—the Retro-Choir with fan vaulting—was built by Abbot Ashton and Abbot Kirton at the end of the fifteenth and at the beginning of the sixteenth century. The elaborate baldacchino over the alter of Derbyshire alabaster was designed by F. L. Pearson, the son of J. L. Pearson, who completed his father's work at Truro Cathedral. At the same time the pavement of Italian marble was laid in the Choir and Presbytery, together with the iron screens enclosing the two eastern bays.

The roof of the Choir is late fifteenth-century, but was restored and redecorated in the nineteenth. In the picture note the lofty triforium, which is a feature of the other Norman Cathedrals of East Anglia at Ely and at Norwich. The Norman arches remain all round the apse on the ground floor and in the triforium and clerestory, but the windows behind them are fifteenth century.

In the south choir aisle are the effigies of former aboots. Two Queens were also buried at Peterborough: Catherine of Aragon (first Queen of Henry VIII) in the north choir aisle beneath the Royal Standards of England and Spain, and Mary Queen of Scots in the south choir aisle; at the west end of the nave is a portrait (an eighteenth-century copy of the original) of the old Sexton who buried them both—Old Scarlett:

Second to none for Strength and Sturdye Limm
A Scarebabe mighty Voice with Visage Grimm.

The body of Mary Queen of Scots was however removed to Westminster Abbey by order of her son, King James I, in 1612 and was reinterred beneath a magnificent monument by Cornelius Cure, Master Mason to the Crown.

Chichester

Cathedral Church of the Holy and Undivided Trinity

THE spire (277 ft high) was rebuilt in 1861 by J. L. Pearson after the fall of the old one built during the episcopate of Bishop William Rede (1369—1385). At the time of rebuilding the tower was raised a little higher, bringing the bases of the belfry windows above the level of the roofs. The picture shows the long, early twelfth-century clerestory to the nave, the inner arches of which had to be rebuilt after the great fire of 1186; only two years after the great church, begin by Bishop Ralph de Luffa in 1091, was consecrated. As part of the repairs carried out after the fire the nave, choir and transepts were vaulted by Bishop Seffrid and the church re-consecrated in 1199.

The original plan provided for two western towers, but both of these had fallen by 1210 and were rebuilt. The northern one fell again in 1634 and remained a ruin until rebuilt by Pearson in 1900. Behind them in the picture can be seen the detached bell tower, or campanile, (1411—1436) in which there is a ring of eight bells, the oldest bearing the inscription *Be mecke and loly to hear the word of God* and was cast by John Watts, bell founder of Salisbury, in 1587.

Appearing in the picture is the circular window in the gable of the south transept, and just below it the head of the magnificent window filled with cur-vilinear tracery which was the gift of Bishop Langton (1305—1377) who lies buried under a canopied tomb just below it.

Winchester

Cathedral Church of the Holy and Undivided Trinity

THE South Transept, illustrated here, is one of the few pieces of Norman work remaining on the exterior of Winchester Cathedral. It is part of the Norman Church commenced by Bishop Walkelin (1070—1098) after the fall of the central tower which damaged the earlier church. The existing tower and the upper stories of the transepts belong to the time when extensive repairs were made during the first half of the thirteenth century. Both the transepts have aisles, those in the south transept being divided by walls and screens to form chapels on the east and a treasury on the west. The house in the foreground of the picture stands on the site of the Chapter House and the picture itself is taken on the site of the Cloister, the east wall of which can be seen between the house and the south transept.

The nave, the eastern end of which appears on the left of the picture, represents part of the vast scheme of reconstruction, encasing and adapting much of the earlier Norman work, by Bishop Edyngton (1346—1366) and his successor, Bishop William of Wykeham (1367—1404).

Winchester Cathedral is the longest in Europe (526 ft). It is longer than St. Alban's by just over five feet, but was exceeded by Old St. Paul's, which was 596 ft in length.

Along the south side of the nave are the massive buttresses which represent part of the extensive measures taken in modern times to strengthen the foundations of the whole building.

Winchester

Effigy of Bishop William of Waynflete

WILLIAM of Waynflete was one of the most notable men in England in the fifteenth century. Of humble origin, the son of Richard Patten of Waynflete in Lincolnshire, he was educated at Winchester School and at New College, Oxford, both founded by his predecessor in the See of Winchester, Bishop William of Wykeham. In 1443 Henry VI made him Provost of Eton and in 1447 he succeeded Cardinal Beaufort as Bishop of Winchester, and in the following year he founded St. Mary Magdalen Hall at Oxford which in 1457 was refounded as Magdalen College. He took a prominent part in the affairs of State and from 1456—60 was Lord Chancellor of England. During the latter part of his life, however, he retired from politics and interested himself chiefly in his educational foundations which included a free grammar school at Waynflete, his native place.

He died in 1486 and was buried in the Chantry Chapel, which he had caused to be made in his lifetime, in the retro-choir of Winchester Cathedral opposite to that of Cardinal Beaufort. His effigy, which is illustrated here, is undoubtedly a portrait and shows him in his vestments: the mitre, the full gothic-shape chasuble folded about the wrists, and the amice, with its wide apparel, round his neck. It rests on a table tomb and tombs of this type often have smaller figures set within the panels all round which are called 'weepers'. The tomb of Bishop William of Wykeham in the nave at Winchester has the figures of three canons as weepers at the foot of the effigy.

William of Waynflete completed the reconstruction of the nave and transepts which had continued for more than a century.

London

St. Paul's

WHEN Sir Christopher Wren designed his new Cathedral he planned a central tower which would be wide enough to cover a big central area at the crossing and at the same time tall enough to be a dominating feature over all London. Thus he designed two domes. An inner dome of brick which was strengthened all round with chains, and an outer dome of wood. Between them is a cone of brick which supports the lantern and the Cross above. The bells are hung in the western towers, the south-western containing the largest—'Great Tom', weighing five tons—which was brought from the Old Palace at Westminster and recast at Whitechapel in 1716.

The impressive west front, with two porticoes one above the other with Corinthian columns set in pairs, has the figure of St. Paul himself in the centre and in the pediment beneath a bas-relief depicting the story of his conversion. The figures on either side are those of St. Peter, St. James and the Four Evangelists.

Commenced in 1675 the choir was completed by 1697 and the whole Cathedral in 1711, the last stone being laid in place by Wren's son. Wren himself died in 1723 aged 91 and lies buried in the south east corner of the crypt beneath the famous inscription:—

Subtus conditur
Huius Ecclesiae et Urbis Conditor
Christopherus Wren.
Qui vixit annos ultra nonaginta
Non sibi, sed bono publico.
Lector, si monumentum requiris
circumspice.